GETTING THE BLUES

THE FUTURE OF AUSTRALIAN LABOR

Nick Dyrenfurth

Published in 2019 by Connor Court Publishing Pty Ltd

Connor Court Publishing Pty Ltd

PO Box 7257

Redland Bay QLD 4165

sales@connorcourt.com

www.connorcourtpublishing.com.au

ISBN: 978-1-925826-67-8

Front Cover Design: Ian James

Printed in Australia

For Lexie, who taught me to love again.

I've got a broken heart and a broken head
I had a little accident
Nothing too serious
Take a look at this place, take a look at this mess
Nothing too serious
If you close your eyes it may go away
Nothing too serious
We can do it again some other day
Nothing too serious
Nothing too serious (is that right?)

Icehouse, 'Nothing too serious', 1987

ACKNOWLEDGEMENTS

This book had its genesis in a workshop of Blue Labour thinkers and politicians held in London during October 2015. I am indebted to its organisers – Simon Greer, Arnie Graf and Lord Maurice Glasman – and many contributors. Numerous colleagues, scholars and friends generously read and commented on drafts of the manuscript or shaped the contours of my thinking and writing over the years. My special thanks to Professor Frank Bongiorno, Michael Cooney, Emma Dawson, Dr Michael Easson, Professor Alan Johnson, Professor Adrian Pabst, Kosmos Samaras, Professor Tim Soutphommasane, Professor Marc Stears, Michael Thompson, and Luke Walladge. All errors of fact or interpretation are mine alone. I owe a special debt of gratitude to Maurice Glasman whose work and tireless activism has been a source of inspiration over the past decade – *Kol HaKavod*. Writing this book would not have been possible without the support of the John Curtin Research Centre. My sincere thanks to its chair and my dear friend, Dr Henry Pinskier, and to all the members of its Committee of Management and Advisory Board, for their support and friendship. Thanks too should go to my friends in the ALP and union movement – rank and file members, staffers, office bearers and parliamentarians – who've endured me and endured the ups and downs of politics and life over the last two decades. I will always be thankful to Bill Shorten for giving me a chance to work in politics – he has much still to contribute to public life. I was fortunate to work with Connor Court in bringing this book to life. Thanks to Anthony Cappello and the team. Finally, thank you to my family for their love, patience and loyalty – even when I scarcely deserved it. I love you all dearly.

Nick Dyrenfurth, Melbourne, 30 August 2019

ABOUT THE AUTHOR

Dr Nick Dyrenfurth is the Executive Director of the John Curtin Research Centre – a Melbourne-based social democratic thinktank. A former academic, Labor Party speechwriter and advisor, Nick is the author or editor of seven previous books, including *A Little History of the Australian Labor Party* (2011, with Frank Bongiorno), *Mateship: A Very Australian History* (2015), *'A powerful influence on Australian affairs': A new history of the AWU* (2017), and *Heroes and Villains: the Rise and Fall of the Early Australian Labor Party* (2011). He is a leading commentator, having written for *The Age, The Saturday Paper, The Australian, Sydney Morning Herald, Australian Financial Review, Daily Telegraph,* and *The Monthly*.

CONTENTS

INTRODUCTION

'What's he bloody smiling about?'

Best to keep schtum: I'm in the throes of what passes for a job interview in politics; as friends joke, making *Aliyah* (right of return) to Labor leader Bill Shorten's office.

It's early 2016 and a storm is whipping Bill's suburban electorate in Moonee Ponds.

There's Bill. Grinning. Making jokes. Almost serene. After *everything*. A politicised royal commission into the trade union movement designed, in large part, to destroy his leadership. Bill's lodestar, his mother Ann, passing away in mid-2014. The spectre of what proved to be false allegations of sexual assault. The Sisyphean task of putting a broken federal Labor Party back together after the historic defeat of 2013. Which Shorten did and more. He saw off one Prime Minister, or rather the 'Prime Minister of the Opposition', Tony Abbott, who never grew in office, only to witness the Messianic arrival of Malcolm Turnbull to the nation's top job in August 2015. The polls reversed course. Bill's enemies smelt blood in the water. The Coalition sensed a landslide ahead. A press gallery whose palpable preference was for the urbane, 'progressive' Turnbull. And a handful of enemies within: Labor's nervous nellies who learnt nothing and forgot nothing of the leadership ructions of the Rudd-Gillard years.

And Bill's grinning. He's hungry for the prize. He exudes destiny. I'm back.

***

Just over three years later, on 18 May 2019, federal Labor was rejected by voters at the ballot box. While the defeat was technically narrow, it was clear that enough Australian voters baulked at its 'progressive' policy offerings and a fundamentally decent centre-left leader in Bill Shorten. 2019 was a clear rejection of Labor's agenda, culture and campaigning. The Coalition did well in most of its marginal seats (losing Gilmore to Labor in NSW and Corangamite and Dunkley in Victoria, with a surprise loss of Abbott's seat of Warringah to an independent Liberal) and won five from Labor (Bass and Braddon in Tasmania, Longman and Herbert in Queensland, Lindsay in NSW) as well as retrieving two seats they won at the previous election – Wentworth (NSW) and Chisholm (Victoria) from independents. Having held a commanding lead in all published polls since mid-2016 and facing a government which had cycled through three prime ministers in three and a half years, it was a shattering defeat for Labor's 'True Believers', but which followed an all too familiar pattern. Since World War Two Labor has won office from Opposition on just three occasions. Twice within the space of twenty years Labor can make the depressing boast of having the best prime minister who never was in two leaders: Kim Beazley and Bill Shorten.

Millions of words will be written analysing Labor's surprise defeat. Some will simplistically blame the leader or campaign headquarters, bad polling, or Labor's 'big target' agenda, notably its so-called 'Retiree Tax' or negative gearing reforms. Others have specifically targeted Queensland and its big spending populist millionaire, Clive Palmer, writing off Sunshine State voters as 'bogans' undeserving of a ballot paper. Many have blamed the Murdoch press and the Coalition scare campaign. Blaming others is an inevitable element of dealing with loss. It will do little to ensure Labor wins an election in three year's time or even presents as a credible opposition.

Labor's recovery must start with the sixty-six per cent of Australians who did not give the nation's oldest political party their first preference vote on May 18. This is roughly the same number, or two-thirds of the populace, who did not vote Labor in 2013 and again in 2016 – that is three elections in a row – most of whom reside in our middle and outer-suburbs and regions. Federal Labor is heading towards the fate of some European social democratic parties – electoral irrelevance. This is a problem that goes beyond one leader, one campaign, one national secretariat or one Coalition government. Labor cannot win national government without changing the votes of a good proportion of these people – in simple terms, it must appeal to people who have not been voting for it for a while. Labor has, to put it mildly, a sizeable problem with a sizeable portion of the federal electorate. Labor's primary vote first fell below 40 per cent at the 1990 election and has never really recovered. By the next federal election due anytime between now and 2022, Labor will have won national government in majority terms just twice in almost three decades: in 1993 when Paul Keating's party won the seemingly unwinnable election, campaigning against the threat of a regressive Goods and Services Tax and the extreme right-wing economic policy agenda more generally proposed by Dr John Hewson's Coalition; and in 2007 when Kevin Rudd took the party back into office largely on the back of the anti-*Work Choices* campaign spearheaded by the union movement. At both these elections, Labor's primary vote was above 40 per cent. Both victories were won on material, 'hip pocket nerve' economic factors, where federal elections are usually won (in 1966 the issue of Australia's involvement in Vietnam clearly assisted the Coalition as did the 9/11 terrorist attacks and MV Tampa issue during 2001). Labor has never won campaigning on its state-level strengths, health and education. The environment has not in itself led Labor into office. If climate change was a factor in 2007 it was because Rudd neutralised the Coalition's advantage in economic management.

Federal Labor's troubles are now at least thirty years old. They are bigger than one person or policy. Modern Labor is the problem, not voters. The first thing Labor MPs and activists – many of whom live in inner cities and have post-tertiary degree careers – ought to do in the election's aftermath and every day until the next election is strike up a conversation with a stranger, preferably outside a 10-kilometre radius of the CBD of one of our major cities. Don't ask them about policy or personalities or what they want from government. Don't ask them about the election or politics or whether they are 'progressive' or 'conservative' or 'left' or 'right'. Ask them what it is they *care about*. They'll almost certainly come back with the same answers. First, they care about their families, and I'm not just talking about nuclear families, but the full spectrum of relationships. How is the marriage? Are the kids ok? What about their ageing parents? Do they have enough to make ends meet? Are they indebted? Second, they care about work: having a job, a job providing enough wages, hours and security, and whether it is meaningful, dignified work. Third, they care about place: community and country. Most Australians – "quiet Australians" as Prime Minister Scott Morrison put it on election night – love their country, they don't want it radically changed unless for good reason. They care about whether their communities are safe from violence, including the threat of terrorism, and care about whether they are well-served by basic amenities and services: childcare, schools, hospitals, transport, and police on the beat. They care about the environment they will pass on to their kids and grandkids, and climate change. They care about how these things will be paid for – about debt.[1]

In 2019, there were parts of Labor's platform that were good, sound economic reforms. But Labor was not trusted to implement them. Why was the party of action on inequality, climate change action, affirmative action, action of an array of quotas, Facebook memes and social media action, and a bastion of progressive thinking, beaten like a drum by a Hillsong Christian who abstained on gay marriage, brought a lump of coal into parliament and leads a party with a 'women problem'. By a prime minister who could not explain why it was he became prime minister in August 2018, then, during the election, or afterwards. The economy, jobs, wages and debt were more important to more Australians. Even when its policy settings are right, the internal culture of the Labor Party and the values it projects are at odds with how many Australians feel. Labor misses this because people feel they shouldn't express their real feelings – so they say the 'correct' thing, agree on climate change or say they're voting on health or education and then in the quiet privacy of voting booths express their true beliefs. A Labor Party that defines itself primarily as 'progressive' will no longer have a broad cultural base of people who can appeal to workers, 'small c' conservatives, non-ideological voters, a diverse middle-class, people of faith, and rural and regional voters – Labor was formed in Balmain *and* Barcaldine after all.

As the Queensland, Western Australian and Western Sydney results reveal, this is a major problem – one that will likely not be fixed by more press conferences or by doubling down on increased government spending, nor spicy climate change rhetoric. Labor won a majority of the two-party preferred vote in a majority of the states and territories – New South Wales, Victoria, South Australia, Tasmania, the ACT and the Northern Territory. Yet the Coalition won 23 of the 30 seats in Queensland and 11 of the 16 seats in Western Australia. The Coalition's thumping majority in those two states was enough to eclipse Labor's majority across the rest of the country. There is a clear path forward for federal Labor – spelt out in an unlikely manner. If Labor listens carefully to the speech given by Scott Morrison on election night therein lies its salvation. The Coalition's victory, Morrison said, was owed to the "quiet Australians". He proclaimed, without reservation: "God bless Australia". If progressives shifted uneasily at the mention of quiet Australians, invoking God must have knocked them out of their seats. It may be the case that Morrison's talk of 'quiet Australians' is as self-serving as John Howard's post-1996 claim to represent working-class 'battlers', yet quiet or not, it is time for Laborites to listen more closely to the Australian people.

Australian Labor's defeat should not be seen in isolation. Most centre-left parties are struggling to define themselves in a world defined by free-market orientated economic globalisation, declining union density and technological disruption. Centre-right parties govern across most of Europe. Jeremy Corbyn's British Labour appears unelectable. Like its social democratic cousins, Australian Labor is increasingly detached from its working-class base of blue-collar and precarious white-collar workers. Its activist middle-class members, many MPs and staffers are increasingly perceived to express the views of a progressive elite. Historically, a labourist party focussed, for the most part, on the material concerns of working Australians, since the 1970s Labor has become an aggressively secular, small 'l' liberal party rattling off progressive policies and talking the language of 'equality', 'diversity' and 'inclusivity'. The divisive, aggravating influence of identity politics – and virtue-signalling – figure too *much* in the rhetoric of Labor activists. Talk of change saturates Labor's thinking and language. It's 'the vibe of it' as *The Castle*'s bumbling lawyer Dennis Denuto might have put it – and Australians aren't feeling it. Too often, Labor's pitch is disconnected from the lives of those to whom the party appeals or should be appealing to.

The truth is Labor has never been and should never be some straightforwardly 'progressive party'. Progressive ideology, while not wrong on many subjects, ranging from the justness of same-sex marriage to acting prudently on climate change, adopts a near Manichean view of the world: black and white, right and wrong. It starts not from where people are, and not by first taking account of things they care most about – family, work and place, but from where progressives would like people to be, in other words, in agreement with progressives. Ironically, progressives, while championing diversity and inclusivity, barely tolerate diversity of thought, notably from religious people. This is an insurmountable roadblock to building a coalition to form national government. The rebuilding of a new cross-class coalition, as this book insists, requires Australian Labor to get a thorough case of the blues, applying to our local context many, but not all, of the ideas of the Blue Labour movement championed by Maurice Glasman, a Labour life peer in Britain's House of Lords. As ex-British Labour MP Frank Field, who left his party of over five decades membership in disgust at the direction of the Corbyn project, writes: "The appeal to country, loyalty to old friends, the belief that duties beget rights, are all sentiments that appeal across classes. It is on this universalism of Blue Labour's common good that Labour should being rebuilding the wider coalition of voters that is so crucial to general election success."[2]

None of the above is rocket science. It is politics 101. Yet some Labor people recoil in horror at these observations. Socially conservative or reactionary, they mutter at the speaker. But if they do this, they betray themselves as fundamentally hostile to the needs and aspirations of the Australian people and what they really care about.

It means they will learn nothing from May 18.

You can have the best policies in the world and still lose. You can have a fundamentally decent party leader and lose. If political parties don't start where people are at, and instead focus on where they'd like people to be, they will lose, every single time. The Australian people are in the right place. Federal Labor isn't. New federal parliamentary Labor leader Anthony Albanese, his colleagues, party members and the entire labour movement must proceed from that basic assumption. This is not a call for Labor to shift to the right, the intellectually lazy fallback of critics who criticise Laborites, across factions, who are urging the party to reconnect with working people. Writing for the edited publication *All That's Left* in 2010 I suggested that a successful political party doesn't merely seek to occupy the centre of politics – it actively shapes the centre in the first place.[3] Former Western Australia premier Geoff Gallop made the case three years earlier. "To win elections political parties need to occupy and successfully manage the centre-ground. Judgement is required because the centre can shift to the right under the pressure of crime, social disorder or international insecurity or to the left because of economic insecurity, social injustice or environmental alarm. To be in the centre may require support for the status quo, it may also mean support for change."[4] Gallop wouldn't put it as such, but this is Labor's social democratic tradition in action: it is both radical and conservative.

Writing in *The Australian*, veteran journalist and historian Paul Kelly remarked of the 2019 election aftermath: "Any prospect the Labor Party will seriously review the source of its election defeat is remote. The reason is simple — there is no will or incentive for a ruthlessly honest review and, given Scott Morrison's narrow win, Labor assumes, no doubt correctly, it will be competitive at the next election. Labor is the party with a history of competitive losses. Being competitive is the substitute for winning. Each defeat holds out the enticing hope of victory next time — and the next time and the next time. It keeps extolling the Whitlam and Hawke legacies in hollow gestures designed to conceal that it is the anti-Hawke party in terms of governance and the anti-Whitlam party in terms of internal reform. Meanwhile, Labor has lost seven of the last nine federal elections — and of the two it won, one was a doomed minority government. Labor has passed a new threshold — the party is beyond reform. And nobody gets angry. Nobody stands up and says 'enough is enough'."[5]

This book says loudly, clearly and, at times, angrily: 'enough'.

***

Getting the Blues is my take on what many are calling Labor's unloseable election and presents a blueprint for movement renewal. It is not only a proposal for internal reform – policy-wise and culturally – but blue in a personal sense. Labor's last six years coincided with a blue period in my own life. It taught me, or retaught, vital lessons in life: of love, loss and loyalty; the meaning of change, security and stability; and the centrality of family, faith, work and community. In 2019, I felt the defeat of the Bill Shorten-led Labor Party intensely. This is my attempt at dealing with the gut-wrenching feeling which defeat wrought upon Labor; an effort to move Labor to a better place. *Getting the Blues* begins by taking stock of the last turbulent decade of Australian politics and identifies what is really roiling our polity – economic insecurity, seismic cultural change and a shattering of faith in our democratic institutions, which, as Chapter Two traces, has led the nation to embrace a debilitating Messiah complex. Chapters Three and Four then provide a candid personal account of the Rudd-Gillard years, the Shorten-era and the 2019 federal election and its aftermath. My account of the election campaign takes the form of a diary – I have only altered it for purposes of style. The final two chapters draw on my writings over the last decade to urge Labor to reconnect with its Labourist traditions – as a reformist party of progress not progressivism – small 'c' conservative disposition and patriotic temper; in short, one that can broker a renewed politics of the Common Good. *Getting the Blues* delves beyond personality politics to provide answers to the big questions confronting Labor: is the ALP fundamentally broken? Will it close its eyes and pretend that decades-long cultural problems will magically disappear? Or does Labor have the willingness to reform and renew as we enter the third decade of the twenty-first century?

1

POTTY POLITICS

Australian politics feels broken, potty even. The BBC has taken to calling our nation "the coup capital of the democratic world."[6] And for good reason. Over the past twelve years Australia has churned through seven prime ministerships, one of whom, Kevin Rudd, returned to office a second time for a little over two months in mid-2013. Between 1983 and 2007, by contrast, Australia was helmed by just three prime ministers: Bob Hawke, Paul Keating and John Howard. The politics of the early noughties is likewise instructive. Across all Australian states and territories and the federal parliament in just one year – 2004 – there was only one change of major party leader, Tasmanian Labor Premier Jim Bacon, who resigned office owing to terminal illness. In the preceding two years, there were three changes per year, each confined to the replacement of the Opposition leader. The trend towards leadership churn has accelerated ever since. No Australian prime minister has served a full term since John Howard's 2004 re-election. Only the gambler with a taste for the long odds would put money on Scott Morrison's victory acting as a circuit-breaker on the prime ministerial revolving-door. Morrison campaigned superbly in 2019; governing is a very different equation. His nine months in office prior to the election were, frankly, lacklustre.

Leaders are no longer guaranteed the privilege of seeing out a term in office or contesting an election as party leader. There have been twenty-eight different premiers and chief ministers of state since 2009, in other words an average of three and a half leaders per legislature for the decade. It is unthinkable that a major party would, as was the case with the federal ALP post-World War Two, be served by leaders of multiple losing elections, in the form of Bert Evatt (1951-60) and Arthur Calwell (1960-67). On one issue – climate change – three prime ministers in a decade have fallen victim to the vicissitudes of public and party opinion; at the 2019 election it was encapsulated by the controversy over the Adani mine in Queensland, cruelling Bill Shorten's chances. So-called 'oncer' governments are increasingly common in the states and territories; three occurring in ten years. It was only a few thousand votes which prevented Gillard Labor (2010) and Turnbull's Liberals (2016) from joining Scullin in the federal pantheon. Once infamous for instability, Italy now appears as an oasis of political calm and parliamentary decorum by comparison with Australia.

Leadership instability begets leadership instability. Rolling opinion polls, a wanton child of the 1990s, frequently contribute to the toppling of elected leaders, creating a vicious cycle which further inclines the public to distrust politicians. Leadership rumours swirl in near perpetuity, cabinets leak like sieves to the media, Treasurers haul chunks of coal onto the floor of parliament, literal fisticuffs occur in Canberra along with rorts and scandal aplenty, and numerous ill-fated 'captain's picks'. Far-Right politicians such as Senator Pauline Hanson use the burqa as an anti-virtue-signalling stunt. No wonder many voters believe that politicians are untrustworthy or worse, more concerned with playing political games, and are consumed by internal machinations, rather than governing or holding the government to account.

What's roiling politics? There is no one moment when politics broke, nor one single explanation for how we got into this malaise. Those who argue it was Labor's dumping of Rudd in mid-2010 which set in train a decade of political misery are mistaken. After all, no credible historian blames the Serbian nationalist Gavrilo Princip's assassination of Archduke Franz Ferdinand for starting World War One. Rather, like the events leading up to the Great War, the roiling of our politics has been incremental and cumulative. The electorate is undoubtedly more volatile and less wedded to the major parties. The majors' share of the vote has fallen precipitously: by twenty percentage points since the 1980s. At the 2019 federal election nearly a quarter of Australians gave their first preference in the lower house to parties other than Labor and the Coalition, essentially replicating the result of the 2016 election, and reflective of a polling trend that has been in the making for decades. Labor claimed a primary vote of 33.3 per cent, effectively its worst result since 1903. The ALP primary vote from the previous three elections was 34.73 per cent in 2016, 33.38 per cent in 2013 and 37.99 per cent in 2010 when it last 'won' installing Julia Gillard's minority government. Having scraped back into office Scott Morrison's Coalition enjoyed a primary vote of 41.43 per cent – its third lowest result in the past sixty years. Its successes in places such as Queensland owed to preferences flowing back from minor parties. Pauline Hanson's One Nation and Clive Palmer's United Australia Party (UAP) had a combined swing to them of 6.7 per cent and fed most of it back to the LNP in preferences. The Senate result for both major parties was full of foreboding. Labor scored a primary of 28.89 per cent nationally. The party's result in Queensland was diabolical: 22.74 per cent, representing a swing against Labor of 3.64 per cent. The Coalition polled just 38.18 per cent. By contrast, Gough Whitlam came to power in 1972 with 49.59 per cent of the lower house primary vote (and lost office after his Dismissal on 42.84 per cent); Hawke garnered 45.15 per cent in 1983; and Kevin Rudd won 43.38 per cent when he won in 2007. The most successful minor party of recent decades has peaked. The post-Bob Brown Greens party has struggled to make any further gains since he retired in 2013: it recorded a lower house primary vote of 10.40 per cent and 10.20 per cent in the Senate, only marginally up on 2016. It is riven by conflict and scandal in the states.

Party poopers

The mythological glory days of the Hawke-Keating 'reform' era and relative calm of the Howard years – explored in detail next chapter – concealed major changes to the way in which we do politics and eroded popular trust in the political system. Political party membership has been in decline since the mid-1950s, when ALP membership peaked at 75,000 members and, in Victoria alone, the Liberals boasted 46,000 members and some 100,000 members nationally.[7] The Liberal's website claims it has more than 80,000 members across more than 2000 branches – it is more likely to sit at around 50,000 members.[8] Labor registered 53,550 members at the end of 2017.[9]

We've changed. Australians are less likely to be joiners – whether it be parties, churches or a host of once-strong civil society groupings. As a result, the major parties have 'hollowed' out in favour of leader-centred, electoral-professional organisations. Indeed, across the English-speaking world, people are walking away from mass parties. In Australia, this is a function of the weakening of a class (and religious) cleavage of Labor versus the rest. This schism dominated twentieth-century politics, one founded on the divide between the manual, Irish-Catholic accented working-class and a largely Protestant middle-class of small business owners and white-collar employees. Since the 1960s, however, class has weakened in terms of tribal identification and party loyalty, and been joined by new flashpoints around education, age, ethnicity, gender and sexuality.[10] The Australian Bureau of Statistics puts total party membership at just 1.3 per cent of the adult population. There are more people on the waiting list to join the Melbourne Cricket Club than members in all parties put together. This is lower than the number of Tasmanian organ donors, many professional football clubs and major unions such as the Shop, Distributive and Allied Employees' Association (SDA).[11]

The electorate has fractured in other ways – around geography, expressed in a 'south eastern corner versus the rest' ethos, between generations and over culture. As George Megalogenis reminds us, it is a new-old divide between those largely metropolitan dwellers who have been winners from globalisation and those residing in outer suburbia and regional and rural Australia who perceive themselves to be on the losing side of its impact on our nation's economic structure and detached from its shifting cultural norms.[12] Economic globalisation, which has uprooted entire industries and offshored working-class jobs, Labor MP Peter Khalil reminds us, has decreased inequality globally, mainly as a result of China and India's growth, but the "global capitalist system in which we live is structurally disadvantageous to the working and middle classes" of the developed world.[13] This trend is bifurcating our nation's politics. Queensland and Western Australia might as well be on different continents than the rest of Australia. An anti-liberal, anti-elite schism is all pervasive, from the United Kingdom's interminable Brexit to the election of the self-styled 'anti-Globalist' Trump. Outside of the West, it is embodied and buttressed by the provincial support base of leaders like Turkey's strongman Islamist President, Recep Tayyip Erdogan.

As political parties shrink, pollies from both sides of the aisle are drawn from a narrower gene pool. Australia, and particularly Labor, has made progress on parliamentary gender representation over the past two decades, certainly in comparison with ethnic and cultural diversity. Yet there are fewer MPs with a background in a manual trade or hailing from a small business occupation. 'Club Fed', as the exclusive club of MPs is sometimes jokingly called, is almost exclusively the home of the university educated. A pre-parliamentary career outside of professional politics is a rarer occurrence as the number of ex-political staffers continues to rise. A recent *Per Capita* study shows teachers – the most common route into federal politics just three decades ago – have been usurped by political operatives. Up to 40 per cent of all MPs and 50 per cent of all Labor representatives have backgrounds as political staffers.[14] These folks aren't bad people – I myself have been a staffer briefly on two occasions – yet their narrower life and occupational experiences less and less reflect the electors they are meant to serve. What's more, a lack of diversity in professional backgrounds leads parties to make decisions, or fail to notice mistakes, potentially alienating voters. Herein lies the paradox of the uber professionalisation of politics: our system is producing fewer skilled practitioners of the art of politics.

It's still the economy stupid!

Dysfunctional politics is as much the symptom as the cause of our malaise. Economic change and popular anger at the growing divide between haves and have nots is the *major* factor roiling political life. Since Federation in 1901, the Australian way of life has been premised on a basic set of assumptions: a fair's day pay for a fair day's work, decent working conditions and job security, a fair say for working women and men in our workplaces and parliaments, in turn, culturally sustained by an egalitarianism of manners, to borrow a phrase from the late historian John Hirst.[15] This way of life was never simply concerned with achieving absolute equality, though equality was a key concern. Nor can it be reduced to some vague 'equality of opportunity' or 'aspirationalism'. Above all, the Australian way was built by working people. It was their efforts and their institutions – unions and the ALP – which created and maintained our national covenant. As the *Per Capita* thinktank's Emma Dawson insists: "Apart from our First Nations people, we are all descended from convicts and immigrants, people whose only assets were their labour, their determination and their resilience. Australia's egalitarian culture was built on a social contract that allowed people to build a good standard of living through their own hard work."[16]

Over the last two decades, however, the Australian Way has been fraying. We are in the midst of a per capita recession. The mining booms of the 2000s and 2010s have changed our economy for the worse. Never before has our economy been less diversified or reliant upon non-renewables to earn us an income in the world or balance the nation's books. The booms encouraged a dangerous short-termism in our thinking, whether in parliament or our boardrooms. While we avoided the worst effects of the global financial crisis and working and middle-class Australians have done better over the past thirty years than most developed countries, notably the United States, inequality has risen to heights not seen since the 1940s. Inequality has rapidly increased over the past six years of Coalition rule. Inequality in Australia is now above the OECD average – the top ten per cent of wealth holders own forty-five per cent of all national wealth.[17] The middle is being hollowed out. A 2019 ABS survey reports that wealth inequality is now at its highest level since the survey began in 1993-94. It shows that high-wealth households increased their average net worth from $1.9 million in 2003-04 to $3.2 million in 2017-18. Over the same period, middle-wealth households increased their average net worth by $148,700. Yet low-wealth households have not experienced any real increase in net worth. Their average net worth of $35,200 in 2017-18 – less than $1000 higher than in 2003-04 – which is equivalent to less than one per cent of all household wealth. As one report of this data suggested, this "disparity has been driven by increases in superannuation balances and the housing market, pushing the average household wealth past the $1 million mark for the first time. The wealthiest households still hold more than 60 per cent of all household wealth, while the middle fifth control 11 per cent."[18] International comparisons bear out these inegalitarian trends. A 2019 OECD report 'Under Pressure', shows that middle-class Australians are being squeezed into lower incomes at some of the fastest rates in the developed world. Australia is a member of an unenviable club of four rich nations – with Britain, the United States and the Netherlands – where there has been a "significant fall" in the number of people on middle and upper-middle incomes.[19]

Good, secure, well-paying jobs are being replaced by low-skill, low-wage insecure work lacking dignity and meaningful career progression. Less than half of Australian workers hold down a full-time permanent job; twenty-five per cent are employed casually, almost double that of the 1980s. The remainder are part-time or labour hire as well as ABN holders, a new precarious tribe increasingly denied job security, sick leave, holiday pay and super – as well as, in many cases, the capacity to borrow or service debt for major investments such as housing. Wages growth has been sluggish for the last six years and the wage share of total income has fallen to its lowest point in over fifty years. While company profits remain healthy, average wages growth is at record low rates and is increasingly decoupled from productivity.[20] The minimum wage in 1983 was 70 per cent of median wages; today it's 55 per cent.[21] Wage theft has become a business model for many corporate entities, though only really eliciting mass attention when it involves celebrity television chefs. According to the Melbourne Institute, data from the Household, Income and Labour Dynamics in Australia survey shows almost a third of casual workers in Australia are earning less than the minimum wage. Thus, with a workforce of 2.5 million casuals, perhaps 350,000 people are being paid below the legal minimum.[22] A full-time job is no protection from economic insecurity. A report by the Australian Council for Social Services shows that 25.9 per cent of Australians in poverty are employed on a full-time basis.[23] Added to this, the gender pay gap remains in Australia, a trend magnified by the disparity between male and female superannuation accounts, impacting women's retirements.[24]

Meanwhile, CEO remuneration and the salaries of our highest-income employees continue to grow at unsustainable levels. Over the past generation, earnings have grown three times as fast for the top tenth of Australian employees as the bottom tenth of workers. Since the early-1990s, average CEO pay in large Australian firms has risen from $1 million to $3 million. The top one per cent share has doubled; the richest 200 Australians have accrued to themselves a rising share of our common wealth and it is growing. Such income inequality is being partially driven by tax avoidance particularly that carried out by multinational companies. The ATO reports that 30 per cent of our largest private companies pay no corporate tax. We are losing $6 billion a year through multinational tax avoidance, money which could be spent on essential services such as health, paying down debt, rolling out nation-building infrastructure and funding our armed services.[25] Is it any wonder Australians are unhappy?

This is to say nothing of those Australians without a job or who are underemployed. Long-term trend employment growth is geared towards the 'gig economy'. Underemployment – employees working but who would like to work more hours – is rising and reached 8.4 per cent in December. The under-utilisation rate — unemployment and underemployment combined — was steady at 13.3 per cent.[26] The correlation between unemployment and underemployment – historically moving in tandem whereby the latter is two points higher than the former – is weakening. The differential is now about three per cent. As economics writer Greg Jericho has warned, this indicates a permanent structural shift towards higher underemployment: bad for young or old Australians, male or female, and especially regional Australia.[27] Youth unemployment, too, is unacceptably high. Youth unemployment sits at around 13.5 per cent; youth underemployment has reached 18 per cent.[28] The omens are poor for job security: a 2015 report by the Committee for Economic Development of Australia estimates that forty per cent of the existing jobs will disappear in the next ten to fifteen years due to technological change.[29] Yet the solution to this structural shift to our world of work is missing: witness our shabby investments in high-tech manufacturing, research and development, and vocational education.

Structural economic change, globalisation and technological disruption were partly unavoidable trends. Yet the decay of

Australian egalitarianism was the result of conscious choices; the pursuit of free market economics over recent decades by governments of all stripes and the collapse of mass unionism cheered on by some on the 'conservative' side of politics. As the former Deputy Prime Minister and Treasurer Wayne Swan argues: "It's no coincidence that both union membership and workers' share of income are at their lowest levels in at least 60 years."[30] This is a global trend. A 2015 International Monetary Fund study of advanced economies identified how the erosion of unionism clearly correlates with increasing income inequality: "the weakening of unions contributed to the rise of top earners' income shares and less redistribution, and eroding minimum wages increased overall inequality considerably."[31] Yet conservatives have as much reason to be alarmed by these statistics as progressives: economic insecurity weakens family and community bonds. The conservative commentator Gray Connolly has observed that a society in which housing is unaffordable will seek out more extreme politics over time.[32]

The fruits of Australia's twenty-eight years of continuous national economic growth have not been shared fairly. According to an Essential Report poll published in late 2016, nearly three-quarters of respondents agreed with the survey's proposition that life for working-class and middle-class Australians has "got worse" or "stayed about the same" "over the last few years".[33] Just five per cent of Australians feel they have personally gained from our record-busting economic run, according to a 2018 Committee for Economic Development of Australia survey. By contrast, 74 per cent believe large corporations have "gained a lot".[34] In any case, our world-beating GDP growth numbers belie a more fragile outlook. Productive investment is poor. Australian exports are badly undiversified in terms of both products and source country. We rely on China to purchase a third of our exports, whose authoritarian government has the ability to damage our economy by rapidly withdrawing investment. Trend line growth is weak. Data from the last national accounts shows the economy grew by

1.8 per cent in the year to March 2019, its weakest performance since September 2009. For the first time since the 1982 recession, per capita GDP – economic growth per person – fell for the third consecutive quarter.[35] Consumer spending is low, as is business investment, yet interest rates are heading towards zero, leaving little room for monetary policy to generate stimulus. Australia's record-breaking run of avoiding recession may not continue. Our economic institutions – capitalism to be precise – are not working in the interests of the majority.[36]

The Australian way is fraying in other respects. The dream of home ownership is slipping away from working Australians, particularly young families. Fewer than thirty per cent of people own their home outright.[37] Those lucky enough to have entered the market are servicing oversized mortgages. ABS data shows that the share of household income going to mortgage repayments in 2015-16 is significantly higher than it was in the 1980s and early 1990s.[38] One in three homeowners are in 'mortgage stress'.[39] Sixty-four federal seats have an above average 'mortgage stress' rating. This phenomenon is replicated across our rental market. Australians are living in private rental for longer. The 2016 census showed 30.9 per cent of households are renting, up from 29.6 per cent in 2011.[40] Unable to buy homes, people are under increasing pressure to pay rent. The Productivity Commission reported that the number of low-income earners living in 'rental stress' increased from 35.4 to 42.5 per cent between 2006 and 2016.[41]

Many of these trends have been evident for years, but the onset of the global financial crisis brutally shook people's trust in democracy, from which we never really recovered. Economic inequality and insecurity are not only materially bad for working people and, as is increasingly appreciated, bad news for the wider economy. Insecurity undermines our democracy, encouraging extremist politics, and opens the door for false prophets, racists and xenophobes. Once thought to have been condemned to the dustbin of history by World War Two, we are seeing a resurgence of extremist right-wing politics. Thirty years on from the Cold War's end, the far-Left is enjoying a strange rebirth – witness the Corbyn/Momentum take-over and apparent ruination of the once great British Labour Party. And yes, a Corbynite would say, 'we have the largest party in Europe and we achieved the biggest increase in Labour's vote since Attlee in 2017', and it is true that the 2017 manifesto was popular because it recognised widespread, inter-generational economic distress and was willing to offer an alternative. Yet the totally dysfunctional Tory government of Boris Johnson is well ahead in the polls. The Corbyn project, to my mind, has no solutions other than a return to 1970s-style statism and fails to grapple with the realities of globalisation, a radically different labour market or the mass entry of women into the labour force. Corbyn's is an old-fashioned, paternalistic response and doesn't offer a new way forward. In any case, the antisemitism crisis within Labour has left many questioning whether it is worth pursuing his agenda if it risks social fragmentation.

Whether its source is from the Left or Right, throughout the West, voters have been highly receptive to demagogic leaders spouting easy solutions, raging against 'elites', and targeting familiar minority scapegoats. The populist revolt is embodied by the sort of nihilistic fury that saw Donald Trump elected in late 2016; it has produced the rolling crises of Brexit in the UK; it is poisoning political debate almost everywhere in the developed world. Australia is no exception. As Adrian Pabst has observed:

> the political contest across the West has descended into culture wars, fuelling the tribalism on which the liberal elites and the insurgents are now thriving. Each side legitimates itself by purporting to protect the public from the threat posed by the other. As a consequence, our politics have become more partisan. Liberal elites dismiss populists as bigots and racists. Hillary Clinton's jibe about Donald Trump voters, many of whom were former Democrat supporters, as a "basket of deplorables" was emblematic of this contempt. Similarly,

insurgents label liberals as "enemies of the people". A once noble newspaper like the *Daily Telegraph* characterises politicians who dissent over hard Brexit as being guilty of treason. As disagreement gives way to demonisation, democracy becomes debased and demagogic.[42]

The other facet of globalisation – the freer movement of people and cultures across borders – is at once the symptom and cause of political toxicity. Migration and multiculturalism have benefitted Australia enormously. It is a great Australian achievement. I am, after all, a product of the post-war program which brought in my Jewish ancestors and Scots, English and Irish before them in the nineteenth century. Labor was the architect of Australia's more diverse immigration policy in the 1940s. It is a testament to the decency and generosity of working-class Australians who accepted the mostly poor migrants and who worked, socialised, inter-married and shared their jobs with the newcomers. Yet the current permissive approach to importing skilled migrants – while propping up the economy in one sense – is having a deleterious effect on working Australians, new and old. Skills formation and training is neglected. The current government effectively rewards those employers who do not invest in the training and development of their own people and future generations. An associated feature of relatively high immigration is the consequences for the wider economy. In parts of the major metropolises, home ownership is becoming unaffordable owing, in part, to excessive demand. The infrastructure and liveability of our cities and suburbs – our schools, hospitals, public transport and roads – have been damaged as a result of chronic under-investment in social and physical infrastructure. Yet it is also the case that poorly planned immigration, a function in part of our federation where the commonwealth sets our migration intake, but state governments foot the bill for new infrastructure and services, is to some extent helping to suppress the wages of local workers, on top of scandalously weak 457 visa requirements – laws which were meant to force employers to prove a genuine skill shortage.

Culturally, this is helping to foment a populist revolt aiding far-Right parties and the Coalition. Rightly or wrongly, many Australians are driven by cultural anxiety, feeling that they no longer recognise Australia as the country they grew up in. In fact, the turn to populist right parties such as One Nation occurs more frequently in ethnically homogenous regions, rather than our melting pot major cities, and is underpinned by economic insecurity. Nonetheless, Labor's tendency is to gravitate between extremes: the party keeps schtum on migration debates for fear of being accused of fostering racism and xenophobia, or engages in fleeting 'we understand you' rhetoric. The latter, as expressed in NSW Labor's recent history of using clumsy language around 'white flight' – describing so-called white 'Anglo' families leaving established suburbs in Western Sydney as migrant families move in – ultimately ended up alienating key blocs of ethnic voters and obscured the real issue: a long-term infrastructure investment deficit, inadequate service provision and resettlement resources.

These trends explain how Labor went to the 2019 election promising a redistributive agenda, but by not building a majority politics capable of addressing economic and cultural insecurity, it was rejected by *enough* swinging voters. As Labor Senator Kim Carr has written of working-class Australian's voting preferences in 2019:

> What does their reluctance to support Labor's reform agenda tell us about our campaign? It says that we paid insufficient attention to the anxieties and insecurities that working-class families have about the future. This is about cultural identity as much as economics. These anxieties were already evident in the 2016 election, when Malcolm Turnbull's enthusiastic spruiking of disruptive change almost wiped out the Coalition's majority. They are a deep-seated reaction to the effects of automation in industry, to stagnant wages growth, and to increasingly precarious employment practices. Above all, they are a response to the effect of all these things on the shifting balance of wealth and power between the inner cities

and the outer suburbs and the regions.[43]

As 2019 evinced, the centre-left have plainly not been the major beneficiaries of economic calamity or cultural change. Social democracy seems in prolonged crisis the world over, out of power in nearly all the developed countries it once dominated, and on life support in former bastions such as Germany. Parties of the centre-right currently govern across most of Europe. Less than twenty years since a majority of Western governments were centre-left, social democrats and socialists are in power in just seven countries which, with the exception of Spain, are all small: New Zealand, Denmark, Portugal, Sweden, Luxembourg and Malta. The demise of PASOK, once the natural governing party of Greece, has spawned a term for the plight of social democratic parties: 'Pasokification'. Social democratic parties have struggled in a post-Cold War world defined by free-market economic globalisation, a severe decline in union density linked to the erosion of blue-collar working-class identity, the rise of the information society and consumerist culture, the breakdown of community-based forms of solidarity resulting from migration and technological changes, and the apparent conquest of mass poverty, at least in the West. For reasons both economic and cultural, working-class voters are less rusted onto centre-left parties, eroding their base vote. Many such parties have a trust deficit as regards economic management and immigration; while their messaging is skewed towards a universalist, highly-secular, rights-centred agenda that struggles to resonate emotionally.

Popular support for traditional social democratic institutions, economic redistribution and, in some places, the welfare state has weakened, even if inequality is on the rise. Despite or precisely because of the conquest of mass poverty, working-class voters in suburban and regional Australia are swinging away from Labor, eroding its core vote over the past decades. "Social democracy", Tony Judt wrote, "has not only come to power in many countries, it has succeeded beyond the wildest dreams of its founders". The electoral decline of social democracy, in his view, was counterintuitive evidence that parties gathered under its umbrella are a "victim of their own success".[44]

Social democracy, as alluded to above, has been destabilised by profound socio-cultural change. We live in a fast-paced, technologically-driven, globalised world alien to the monocultural, racially exclusive, male-dominated Australia of the twentieth century. On the one hand, greater gender equality, more tolerant attitudes towards sexual preference and ethnic diversity are to be welcomed, yet the demise of monocultural Australia has fractured taken-for-granted forms of social solidarity here as elsewhere. Tight-knit, geographically-fixed communities have crumbled under the weight of revolutionary changes in communications (such as the Internet) and other techno-scientific innovations (human mobility within and beyond nations). Some call this social atomisation, others the loss of social capital, the sense that citizens are 'bowling alone': we are more reluctant to be joiners and know our neighbours less and less. Whatever its nomenclature, hyper-individualism strikes at the heart of social democracy: the desire and very means to collectively better one's society.

Technological change is also transforming the practice and the reportage of politics. Mainstream media sources have declined. Print media is in a death spiral. People's potential sources of news are multiplying – there has never been greater choice and yet the tendency of online readers is to retreat into silos. Social media and the rise of the 24-hour media cycle are having a distinctly asocial effect on politics. Anonymity inspires uncivil discourse less likely to manifest itself in the real world. Debate is grossly simplified, and group-thought unconstrained in the age of memes and Twitter pile-ons. What happens on Twitter has not stayed on Twitter. As the journalist Hugh Riminton noted upon Turnbull's departure: "Perhaps it is coincidental, perhaps not, but no Australian prime minister has served a full term since

#Twitter was invented."[45] The speeding up of Australian politics has qualitatively changed the way policy is conceived, developed, prosecuted and implemented. It is common for a government to announce a policy or policies, often with little or no consultation fearing a drawn-out public stoush over the finer details, and then dump said policy in the face of raging social media armies, noisy vested interests or to appease jumpy backbenchers worried about losing their seats. As the media cycle intensifies, fewer Australians are truly engaged with politics, Peter Lewis, Executive Director of Essential Media notes, "[T]he structures that underpin our democracy are getting weaker. Fewer people consume news. Fewer people trust their public institutions. Fewer people think politicians represent their interests," he writes. "As interest wanes, politics makes more noise to be heard, only to further alienate the public in the process. This creates a climate for easy solutions and hero figures to come in and clean up the mess."[46]

Babies of the house

The speeding up of politics is not confined to the news cycle. Our politicians disdain ageing gracefully. Historically, most MPs and Senators have been elected to parliament in their late thirties and forties, that is, after one or two or three careers. But from Europe to the United States and Oceania, the last decade has seen politicians elected at an earlier age, often in their early 30s and sometimes 20s, and spinning out of parliament at an alarming pace. Politics is more frequently a first career. Granted, precocious young political talents are nothing new: prominent MPs have been elected early in life including Prime Ministers Malcolm Fraser and Paul Keating who were both elected at age 25 in 1955 and 1969 respectively. Chris Watson was Australian Labor's first prime minister – and the first Labo(u)r or social democratic PM in the world – having been sworn in at 37 in 1904. William Pitt the Younger, British Tory statesman of the late-eighteenth and early-nineteenth centuries, became the youngest UK Prime Minister in 1783 at 24. Yet, there is a global youth trend at work today: right-wing Austrian Chancellor Sebastian Kurz is Europe and the world's youngest head of state and his country's youngest ever, elected age 30 in 2017. France's Emmanuel Macron who started up his *En Marche* party as one would a new café or i-Phone App, became President aged 39 in 2017. Italy's Deputy Prime Minister, Luigi DiMaio, from the controversial populist right-wing Five Star movement, arrived to the job at 31, after entering parliament four years earlier. Mhairi Black, a Scottish Nationalist Party MP, was first elected at the age of 20 in 2015 – making her the youngest-ever MP to serve in the House of Commons since 1832. In the United States, Democrat Rep. Alexandria Ocasio-Cortez – 'AOC' in Twitter-speak – became the youngest woman elected to Congress at age 29. In Australia, the LNP's Wyatt Roy was elected to federal parliament age 20 in 2010, the youngest ever. New Zealand Labour PM Jacinda Ardern swept to power aged 37, after less than nine years in the national parliament.

Politicians come and go from leadership positions with unseemly haste. As I write, Ardern's leadership is riding a wave of popular acclaim in and outside of New Zealand in the wake of the Christchurch terror attack on two mosques. The example of Canada's self-styled youthful rockstar Prime Minister Justin Trudeau should, however, caution taking for granted her political immortality. Ardern leads a minority government after all. British Labour's Ed Miliband became opposition leader aged 40 and vacated the position after losing the 2015 election. His Tory vanquisher, David Cameron, came to the British Prime Ministership at 43 and was out of the job before his fifties began. Australia has not been immune to this trend. The median age of an Australian Prime Minister on the first day of their first term is 52 years and 353 days, and most of our recent leaders have come to high office around this age. Yet the speed with which they are arriving in parliament and attaining the prime ministership is accelerating. Howard and Keating served in parliament for twenty-two years each before claiming the top job. Of the next five prime ministers after Howard only Tony Abbot came to close to serving such a parliamentary apprenticeship and, in his case, it counted for little. Three of the five were politicians for ten or less years: Rudd (nine), Turnbull (seven) and Morrison (ten), while Julia Gillard was just shy of twelve years.

Part of the explanation for what Patrick Weller once called the 'younging'[47] of politics lies with the relentless mental and physical demands placed on politicians by the news cycle, intrusive media, on top of the travel and time spent away from family and friends necessitated by the asocial work environment of Canberra. This structural shift is seen most dramatically in the political staffer class, which, like many MPs, is more middle-class, and more post-material in values and outlook than the rest of the electorate. Parliament House is no country for old men or women. Tech-savvy middle-class millennials have come to dominate its ranks on all sides of politics. Most political staffers are aged in their mid-20s and early 30s and are free of the demands placed on them by young families and long-term relationships. They make the journey from university and involvement in student politics to (often simultaneously) working as an electorate officer or staffer and, often enough, the life of an MP in rapid succession. NSW Labor's general secretaryship, one of the most powerful organisational roles in the party nationally, has been occupied by two (very talented) twenty somethings in the 2010s – Sam Dastyari and Kaila Murnain. Alistair Jordan was just 29 when he became Rudd's second chief of staff in 2008. According to legend, Rudd, demanded that all his political staffers be aged under thirty upon becoming prime minister.

Surveying the age of staffers is not to suggest they are less intellectually able or innately less politically skilled or even bereft of public policy nous. Their views are especially important given the generational divides opened up by the changing nature of our economy, automation, technological disruption, housing affordability and climate change. Not for a moment do I mean to let badly behaved older middle-aged men off the hook. Yet, by definition, younger staffers have not acquired the life experiences and perspective which comes with age – the achievements but also the disappointments we accumulate over the course of our working lives. They are arguably more at risk of succumbing to groupthink, notably that with an inbuilt post-material bias, or less able to stand up to a leader's wants or whims, even though they may be right. Through no fault of their own they are trapped inside what some describe as the 'Canberra bubble', when their own bubble has yet to burst; that is, before their own experience of failure, a necessary precondition of giving advice.

It's not them, it's us

This is not an exercise in nostalgia or an argument for an unrepresentative parliament of the geriatric and infirm. Yet it is the clear that our political class, as a whole, has become part of the problem of our un-virtuous cycle. As George Megalogenis points out, during the past decade Australia has had no substantial reform introduced that's survived a change of government, with the notable exception of Julia Gillard's National Disability Insurance Scheme.[48] It cannot be that every flagship policy has lacked merit or contained a fatal flaw. Short-termism, expediency and the mobilisation of vested interests and those who are winners from existing structures, rather, are trumping long-term policy development. Policy which looks over the political horizon is easy prey for social media hunters, driving policy-on-the-run and leadership churn.

Perhaps too, we the Twitterers, we the consumers of Facebook feeds, we the electorate must share a portion of the blame. Voters the world over are exhibiting disillusionment towards mainstream parties and are increasingly distrustful of democratic institutions more broadly, a trend borne out in Australia. The Australian National University's Australian Election Study has tracked a steady fall in voter satisfaction with democracy, from 86 per cent in 2007 to 60 per cent at the 2016 election, its lowest ebb since the aftermath of the dismissal of the Whitlam government in 1975.[49] Mistrust, apathy and cynicism are leading us into dark places. The Lowy Institute's annual poll has revealed a severe complacency about democracy. In 2018, it found that only 47 per cent of Australians aged 18-44 agreed that "democracy is preferable to any other kind of government."[50] Politicians are regarded with barely concealed contempt, on a par with used car salesmen. But what if our retreat from organised politics – 'show business for ugly people' – has contributed to this malaise? What if our expectations of what our Canberra-based politicians can actually deliver are unreasonable? What if it's us, not the pollies?

Some argue that Australian politics is potty for these reasons. They allege we've never had it so good, despite our lacklustre political class and an ungrateful public. In 2018 *The Economist* magazine lauded our nation as a beacon of the developed world:

> Rising incomes, low public debt, an affordable welfare state, popular support for mass immigration and a broad consensus on the policies underpinning these things—that is a distant dream in most rich countries. Many Western politicians could scarcely imagine a place that combined them all. Happily, they do not have to, because such a country already exists: Australia ... its economy is arguably the most successful in the rich world. It has been growing for 27 years without a recession—a record for a developed country.

For good measure *The Economist* bemoaned the nation's killing of the golden goose:

> The irony is that, just as the benefits of this set-up are becoming so obvious, Australians appear to be growing disenchanted with it ... Politicians, conscious of voters' disgruntlement, have also become increasingly febrile. They are constantly turfing out prime ministers, in the hope that a new face will

boost their party's standing with the electorate ... Ambitious reforms have become rare. The rest of the world could learn a lot from Australia—and Australians could do with a refresher course, too.[51]

Inadvertently, given its rose-tinted glasses view, *The Economist* reminds us not to overstate the current crisis of politics. First, we've been here before. In the federation decade we had eight prime ministerships and ten until 1915, six in the 1940s, and another five in the seven years from Menzies' resignation in 1966 to the end of 1972. Even then across the 118 years since Federation, Australia has had thirty prime ministers, or an average of one for just under every four years – Malcolm Turnbull's reign between 2015 and 2018, then, was about on statistical average. Second, we are not in the throes of a return to the political hatred and social conflict of the 1930s Great Depression, not yet at least. Frequent changes of prime minister have not sparked violent rallies or calls to revolution. Our adversarial parliamentary system is working in part as designed: institutionalising political conflict and disagreement rather than spurring political bloodshed. The sound and fury of Canberra doesn't signify altogether nothing: much work, bipartisan even, transpires behind the scenes, in committees and on the floor of parliament. It's just not reported. Third, we might just be on the cusp of a renewed politics. Often enough, periods of political turmoil ushered in eras of long-term bipartisan reform whether the Menzian economic 'golden era' or the Hawke-Keating Labor governments of the 1980s and 1990s.

Even then a fuzzy political nostalgia means we are inclined to forget the swashbuckling policy debates within and without the major parties, and internal treachery and leadership dramas we only later understood to be 'consensus'. It is delusional to think a bipartisan ceasefire is in the offing or that we will enter the political kingdom of Kumbaya. Democracy is an exercise in imperfection. There is no upgrading to the i-Politics model X when the latest contract expires. Yet this is precisely what we expect of changing governments or prime minister. The prime ministerial revolving door is the product of our Messiah complex – a national disease, if not an epidemic – which, unless cured, offers perpetual disappointment.

2

MESSIAH COMPLEX

"The past is a foreign country: they do things differently there". So runs the famous first line of L.P. Hartley's novel *The Go-Between*. Nostalgia, critics insist, is clouding our judgement of the state of modern politics, which has not 'worsened' over time. Rather we underestimate the messiness and partisanship of previous eras, and the frailties and missteps of previous national leaders. Labor's Shadow Treasurer and Gen X thought-leader Jim Chalmers termed this 'Austalgia' in a 2015 essay in *Meanjin*, a kind of political homesickness for the past which "threatens the political system's ability to put one foot in front of the other" and "holds us back from dealing with the challenges of the future".[52] Certainly, political Austalgia can blind us to the sliding doors moments of even our best prime ministers. What if, for example, Gough Whitlam lost the Labor leadership in 1968, instead of narrowly surviving a challenge from Jim Cairns, or Bob Hawke not replaced Bill Hayden on 1983 election eve, or been turfed from office in the close-run, snap election he called as prime minister in 1984? Both would have been remembered very differently in our popular imagination, or that of Labor's. In any case the modernising projects that Whitlam and Hawke each initiated and represented were greater than one leader. They won support by coalition building from within the labour movement. Hawke, particularly, achieved success with the union movement's critical backing via The Accord. Similarly, in our time, to break the current impasse, we must resist any utopian, self-defeating belief that we are just one Messiah away from returning to 'normal', that a change of prime minister can magically fix the economy, a cure for all ills of modern politics. It's the team that's needed, the ideas to drive them, not just the superb leadership skills of an exceptional person.

They've got personality

Political honeymoons never last, but there is something different about the disposability of modern leaders. How did we get here? For reasons outlined earlier, increasing numbers of voters are deserting the major political parties. As a partial result, Australian politics has grown more personalised and presidential in recent decades, even if the underlying structures of our 'Washminster' system – combining elements of Britain's Westminsterism and the US's system of government – have not fundamentally altered. Parties increasingly craft campaigns around the personality of leaders. In tandem, media coverage of politics tends to frame issues, polls and electioneering in terms of individuals. On one hand, this focus on leaders as message bearers for their parties makes sense – its easily digestible and, for the most part, leaders embody majority internal party opinion. As the *Guardian*'s Jonathan Freedland noted a few years ago: "Personalities do matter. They are in fact the way we human beings understand and process politics. Look no further than the place routinely bashed as the home of personality politics: the United States. Presidential races come alive when individuals step forward to embody what would, without them, be abstract ideas."[53] On the other hand, personality becomes a dangerous fetish when policy is subsumed by a preoccupation with leader personality – from their fashion choices to sex lives and preferred 'democracy sausage' eating techniques. Fetish or fashion, party leaders are perceived as essential to electoral success. Leaders who don't deliver at the ballot box, or in nonstop opinion polls asking respondents to nominate a preferred prime minister or opposition leader, are terminated with extreme prejudice.

Personality fetish means our understanding of political instability is less informed by what is really driving the long-run institutional behaviour of the major parties, the underlying health of the economy and its impact on electoral fortunes, and leadership dynamics beyond gossip or tittle-tattle. As Monash University academics Paul Strangio and James Walter demonstrate in their 2007 book *No, Prime Minister: Reclaiming Politics from Leaders*, the centralisation of power in Canberra and the PMO actually began with Gough Whitlam's reformist Labor government (1972-75).[54] In the long-run, this owes to the hollowing out of the major political parties, institutions which once acted as a brake on the will of domineering leaders and prime ministers.

There have been significant changes in the nature of the public sector, notably the politicisation of the role of public servants which the Howard government ushered in with sackings of a number of departmental heads in 1996, and institution of five-year contracts. From that point on, public service expertise, advice and standards have been eroded, ultimately to the detriment of the parties in power. 'Frank and fearless advice' is more likely to appear in the Museum of Australian Democracy than in the offices of the government of the day or its executive. Public servants say as much. According to an Institute of Public Administration Australia survey of current and former public servants, almost half said their institutions had become more political; the majority said ministerial advisers played too great a role in governance (60 per cent), and 70 per cent thought the same of consultants. Just 30 per cent believed that the public service remained "frank and fearless".[55] And yet the centralisation of decision-making power is a form of self-harm; faux-ascendancy over colleagues and public servants produces poorer quality, short-term focussed decision-making. As our recent experience shows, it can lead to paralysis and leadership coups.

Two examples prove the point. Rudd's demise as prime minister was sheeted home to his manic work habits and incivility. At the time, I thought this a decisive reason for change. But the consequences have been deeply troubling for Labor. And I am troubled by a comment attributed to a legendary Labor warrior and speechwriter, Graham Freudenberg. When he died last July one of his friends posted: "Of all the memories, one that stays with me was in the aftermath of Rudd's removal. Dad and I were sitting with him in the foyer of the Rydges [Hotel] in Kings Cross, and I was arguing the case for it. Reflecting on a certain former employer of his, he said: 'If I were to recount for you every tantrum, insult, slight, jibe and Prima Donna act, I could draw for you a monster. And it wouldn't be the person I knew'."[56] However, in the period of his ascendency, Labor activists were inclined to downplay the significance of Kevin07's 'outsider' antipathy to Labor-style collectivism, that he was not, like Hawke, Keating and even Beazley, a creature of the labour movement. This was made flesh by Rudd's decision to unilaterally overturn a century of ALP tradition during the 2007 election campaign, when he removed the power of caucus to choose the incoming ministry. Rudd's authoritarianism in office built on this original sin. As Prime Minister he ran roughshod over established cabinet and caucus processes designed to facilitate coherent and collegial governance, which contributed to some of his administration's erratic policy decision-making and fuelled internal anger. Paul Strangio has written: "Neither constrained by his party nor chastened by experience, Rudd gave licence to his worst traits as prime minister." Rudd's fall illustrated the "fragility of a leader who relies on a personalised mandate" and who "rules around rather than through their own party ... They are likely to have few genuine allies and survival depends on maintaining support in the fickle opinion polls. This in itself weakens governance and once their electoral Midas touch fades their party is unlikely to be sentimental ..."[57]

Likewise, explanations of Tony Abbott's downfall in 2015 were focussed on personality. The then PM's consumption of a raw onion became an online sensation, as did his penchant for 'budgie smugglers' – meaning that the shaky nature of the economy was neglected. Observers were more attuned to the PMO's centralisation of power during Abbott's error-prone leadership, but that too was reported through the lens of personality, especially the high-profile role of his chief of staff, Peta Credlin.

The rise and fall of Rudd and Abbott laid the groundwork for the cult of personality which greeted Malcolm Turnbull's Prime Ministership in September 2015. Once more the public and much of the commentariat came to believe that one man could 'save' Australian politics, in the process failing to take seriously more systemic issues at play and ignoring Turnbull's Ruddesque-like leadership qualities. Our politics arguably entered the realm of insanity: we were doing the same thing over and again and expecting a different result. Australia is not alone. A similar pattern has been exhibited by parallel democracies: Canada's Justin Trudeau and to a lesser extent Barack Obama are two examples of leaders hailed as messiahs by their respective electorates only to disappoint voters when it turned out they were, in fact, human after all.

The voting public cannot escape censure. It is our limited political attention spans – no matter the demands of work, family, multiplicity of news sources or pollie spin – which are driving dumbed down three-word slogans and personality politics. We have been drawn to charismatic leaders only to grab the remote and switch channels when their fortunes dip. We have over-invested in leaders knowing that one man or woman cannot singlehandedly turn the tide of history. We saw it in Kevin Rudd – who at one stage was the most popular PM in our history according to polling – only to proclaim, 'The King is dead, long live Malcolm!' It is we voters who have been swayed too easily by ephemeral polling popularity. And it is we voters who have been too impatient for the next big leadership thing – pushing leaders who came to the job too early such as Mark Latham or those temperamentally ill-equipped for leadership (Rudd, Abbott and Turnbull, Latham again). Is it any wonder that our messianic leaders fail?

A further problem with our longing for some messiah to 'fix' politics and, more generally, our fixation with Canberra-based politics, is its exaggeration of the ability of governments of all ideological stripes to generate meaningful reform. Two decades of government-led deregulation (some worthwhile, much not), the effects of globalisation, and media flux/technological disruption, have made the task of national government harder by definition. In any case, governing the Commonwealth of Australia has never been easy, given the constitution's checks on the scope of federal power in favour of pesky state governments – the ones who actually deliver most of the essential services we take for granted – and frequently obstructionist senates. Most importantly, political Messianism flies in the face of deep historical experience.

***

He's not the Messiah …

"Whose party is this - ours or his?" was a famous call to arms during the 1968 federal Labor leadership showdown.[58] Issued by Gough Whitlam's left-wing challengers, their rallying cry sought to tap into caucus resentment at his supposedly autocratic tendencies. Whitlam survived and, depending on the judge, tempered his habits. Yet the experience underscores why Labor, in particular at the federal level, has enjoyed an unhappy relationship with Messiahs. (An exception, arguably, at the state level was NSW Labor leader Jack Lang, who disastrously split the labour movement and contributed to the Scullin government's fall. Lang was Messiah turned Golem for those who opposed his leadership.) For most of its history, Labor adopted a sceptical attitude towards leaders, its collectivist impulses wary of the will to dominate of its leaders. Theoretically, Labor leaders boasted the same status as any other member of the party, often to their chagrin. In 1905, for instance, Chris Watson (Labor's first PM for three months the previous year) threatened to resign the leadership if he was to be "given no greater voice" in the selection of ministers in a

Labor government "than the rawest recruit in the party".[59] The party's leadership scepticism was soon warranted. Following Andrew Fisher's resignation as wartime prime minister in late 1915, Labor's federal caucus unanimously elected Billy Hughes as his replacement. Hughes's elevation owed, in part, to a belief that he alone could salvage the drifting government. "Unquestionably he is a great man", crowed the *Australian Worker* newspaper, "with great services still to perform for Australia."[60] Within the year however Hughes split the party when he wilfully sought to introduce military conscription. Labor was subsequently exiled from power for a generation. The *Worker* turned on "Billy". A conspiratorial clique of capitalists found their "Judas ... and he occupied the position of Labor's most honoured servant".[61] Therein lay the rub: he had not been treated as a servant but a Messiah. It was a lesson Labor turned to scripture.

At least until the late 1960s, the ALP mostly avoided succumbing to political messianism. From that time on, however, Labor's salvation has appeared ever more conditional on a transformative leader in the mould of a Whitlam or a Hawke. The complex is like a political sugar-high. The initial euphoria cultivates wholly unrealistic expectations and when reality hits supporters are inevitably disappointed. In 2003, faced with the Howard ascendancy, Labor turned to Mark Latham for its salvation. Simon Crean became the first Labor leader in its history to be denied the chance to fight an election. Latham, having led Labor to a heavy defeat at the 2004 election, imploded after the campaign, after which he resigned in spectacular fashion. The lessons of the Latham experiment were soon forgotten with the appearance of a self-styled messiah known as Kevin 07. Kim Beazley was dispatched by his colleagues in favour of the Rudd/Gillard 'dream team' during late 2006, despite the fact that Beazley-led Labor Party's primary vote hovered around 40 per cent for most of 2005 and 2006. Rudd brought Labor in from the electoral wilderness at the 2007 election and appeared unassailable until early 2010. Yet his downfall in mid-2010, while a product of his abrasive, unilateral leadership style and policy shortcomings, also owed to a belief that his deputy Julia Gillard might be Labor's latest Messiah. Gillard and Rudd enjoyed honeymoons in the polls before inevitably crashing back to earth. It was so sadly predictable. Turning to Gillard and back to Rudd in 2013 did not solve Labor's deeper crisis of political identity and purpose. In this reading, Rudd's celebrity ways were a symptom and not the cause of Labor's leadership instability and fruitless search for a salvation through a new Messiah. (Although it might be noted that in his second coming as ALP leader and prime minister, Rudd was no longer a Messiah figure. It was a purely transactional bargain, to reduce the extent of inevitable electoral carnage.)

Leadership coups also have the effect of smashing what mandate a leader-driven party came to office with and calls into question the judgment of the parties which made them leader in the first place. Victor and vanquished are stripped of authority, notably in the case of Turnbull kowtowing to his party's Right. And while the public might be attracted to the idea of a Messiah, the evidence is clear: every coup since 2010 has been punished with a swing against the government. As George Megalogenis notes, Gillard and Turnbull suffered almost identical swings come election time. Labor lost 11 seats under Gillard in 2010; the Coalition lost 14 under Turnbull in 2016. Scott Morrison's surprise victory in 2019 ostensibly bucked this trend, but it was a narrow victory and certainly not a wholehearted embrace of the Coalition's threadbare agenda.[62]

Ironically, it was one of Rudd's parting gifts to the Labor which may have killed off, for the time being at least, its Messiah complex. His unilateral changing of the rules to the way Labor elects its leader federally (replicated in some states), rammed through caucus in July 2013 upon return to the prime ministership, gave ALP members an equal say with caucus members in deciding the leader. Rudd's rules made it a tougher task to switch leaders on a whim. The leader can only be subject to a leadership ballot with the approval of 60 per cent of caucus and 75 per cent if the leader is elected prime minister. In doing so it upped the transactional costs of leadership changes between elections – and literal cost given the need for a formal ballot of members. Shorten's leadership benefitted from such stability, notably when under pressure after Turnbull's ascension. Yet Shorten's Hawke-like consultative, group leadership was well suited to the times, as Labor sought to heal itself after the tribulations of 2007-13. Seeking the leadership, he explicitly contrasted himself with Rudd, saying: "I'm here today to declare that the era of the Labor Messiahs needs to come to a close."[63]

Shorten's leadership also threw into relief Labor's other debilitating psychological ailment in the post-1996 era.[64] Since 2013, Labor has in some ways been more open to a genuine contest of ideas within its ranks, and ideas from sister parties and like-minded thinkers locally and intellectually. Some thinkers have sought to reckon with Labor's '1983 and all that' moment. To borrow a phrase from British Labour figure Lord Maurice Glasman, the Hawke-Keating Labor governments (1983-1996) became, for many MPs and others, the 'platonic ideal' of a reformist Labor administration by means of floating the dollar, deregulating parts of the economy and privatising government assets. But where Tory Margaret Thatcher carried out this agenda in the United Kingdom by attacking unions, Labor worked with them via the 'Accord' and by means of implementing a 'social wage' (Medicare and superannuation). Through an emphasis on prudent economic management, national consensus and orderly decision-making, Hawke managed to avoid the fate of Whitlam (controversially dismissed by the Governor General in 1975 after three years in office).

Shorten's and Labor's defeat highlights that the ALP's '1983 and all that' view remains a repressive force in two ways. First, the party in government, as seen between 2007 and 2013, struggles to live up to those herculean standards and, second, an overweening deference to that era blocked the path to philosophical and policy renewal. Beginning with the ascent of Whitlam in the 1960s, hastening under Hawke-Keating, but reaching its apotheosis during the Rudd-Gillard era, Labor placed too much faith in the ability of free markets guided by increasingly centralised government to solve society's problems. In short, Labor embraced a bloodless form of wonky, statist liberalism – economic and social – at odds with its original purpose and a language expressive of the basic human aspiration of leading a good, secure and meaningful life: the very reason Labor was put on this earth, something examined in Chapter Five. Post-May 18, the Labor cry has emerged afresh: be more like Bob and Paul.

None of this is to argue that these governments did not change Australia for the better. We are wealthier, more open and dynamic because of them. There is a real sense in which the Hawke era of the 1980s, as Jim Chalmers puts it, was a "golden era", though one adept at claiming successes rather than shortcomings: "There's no denying our democracy did reach a kind of peacetime peak in the years following the 1982 recession. Hawke was cunning, Keating was brave, the Cabinet was clever, the bureaucracy was strong; long overdue changes came in a rush and then changes no-one had thought of followed hard on their heels. Somehow, responsibility for the 1991 recession evaporated with the years; a final tribute to the political deftness of this remarkable generation."[65] To be sure, long-dead governments could not have written Labor's 2019 election policy manifesto or future manifestos. Whitlam, Hawke/Keating and even Rudd/Gillard were a product of their times. The mobile phone and internet-free era of 1983 is no longer a neat guide to our globalised world. An electoral pitch along the lines of 'Let's do what Bob and Paul did' is as plausible as convincing a newly-minted P plate driver to buy a Melways in preference to using Google maps. Even Paul Keating has in recent times admitted that the neo-liberal economic philosophy he championed as treasurer has "run into a dead end".[66]

***

It is not just Labor that has cultivated a self-destructive Messiah complex. The disillusionment produced by the Abbott prime ministership led Liberals, large sections of the public and commentariat to embark on the search for a new messiah of their own. Malcolm Turnbull, in particular, was routinely touted as the urbane, sophisticated and 'progressive' leader who might restore faith in politics. Frenzied excitement occasioned his every leather-jacketed appearance on the ABC's *Q&A* or latest poll with him as preferred Liberal leader. When the moment came in September 2015 for Turnbull to topple Abbott citing the loss of thirty Newspolls in a row, it felt as if the one-time denizen of Nazareth had returned. "We are at the beginning of a new era in Australian politics", cheered former Howard cabinet minister Amanda Vanstone writing in *The Age*. "For the first time in ages, when my mind turns to politics I have both high hopes and a happy heart." Mal Brough, the new Special Minister of State, said this of the new PM: "The smile on Malcolm Turnbull's face, the body language is as important as what he is saying because people want to be uplifted, they want to feel that they can embrace the future and there is a vision there to do that."[67]

The ascension of Turnbull to the prime ministership confirmed the messianic appetite of the political class, media outlets and voting public – along with immense relief at seeing the back of Abbott.[68] Yet, as was the case with Rudd, messianism concealed the innate leadership weaknesses of a man who was not a tribal Liberal, who was ultimately not a creature of the party, despite or precisely because of his largely self-made millions or his mannerisms and speech or high culture tastes. Yet, as a few commentators warned at the time, there were unnerving similarities with Rudd's rise to the prime ministership. Turnbull was heavy on 'big picture' motherhood statements, yet always light on concrete policy details. His promises to restore proper cabinet government and party-room debate – he made the fatal mistake of overpromising in the first flushes of becoming leader – ran contrary to a lifetime's leadership style within and without politics. A long-run appraisal of Turnbull's leadership and temperament, as leader of the Australian Republican Movement in the 1990s, and in his first stint as Opposition Leader (2008-09) revealed a penchant for autocratic captain's picks, a disdain for those he considered intellectually inferior, and a fragile temperament ill at ease with party discipline, personal setbacks and the grimier aspects of day-to-day politics. While he blamed John Howard for 'breaking the heart' of Australians by virtue of campaigning against an Australian republic at the 1999 referendum, Turnbull's own leadership bore some responsibility. His performance as Opposition leader was a divisive, chaotic era punctuated by the dreadful judgment he exhibited during the 'Utegate' affair, when he relied upon the falsified email of the partisan public servant Godwin Gretch. Facing or having suffered defeat or under pressure, Turnbull was prone to exposing how rattled he was by lashing out or overreaching. And few would describe Turnbull's previous roles as a cabinet minister as the pinnacle of quality public policy making. There was always the very real prospect that Turnbull would not be granted a clean run at the prime ministership. The ideological divisions and personal animosities that characterised the post-Howard Coalition were not so easily healed, to say nothing of the personal angst of the deposed Abbott. It was always difficult to believe that Turnbull, who turned 61 shortly after becoming prime minister, could break the habits of a lifetime.

Part of the problem lay with the media's reception of Turnbull. His ascension was complicated by the fact that many journalists generally shared his cosmopolitan ideological worldview, combining progressive social values with an adherence to free market economics. And for all Turnbull's talk of 'exciting times', the 2016 election and the fate of his prime ministership were always going to be determined on the basis of the economy. Anxiety and fear proved more apposite markers of the electorate's mood than Turnbull's rhetoric of hope and optimism. "It's all very well to go on with this spiritual stuff", the successful NSW Labor premier Neville Wran lectured Bob Hawke in 1983 as the aspirant PM set about winning office on the back of his slogan, 'Recovery, Reconciliation and Reconstruction', but it sounded "like a meeting of the fucking Hare Krishnas ... Give them something to vote for. These greedy bastards want a quid in their pockets."[69] Hyperbole, yet economic self-interest, broadly conceived, almost always trumps feel-good post-material politics. This is especially the case when the Messiah happens to be a multimillionaire bankrolling his party's campaign.

The corollary to the Liberal search for a messiah is a fawning nostalgia for John Howard's 11 and half year old Coalition government, one dispatched by voters twelve years ago.[70] A section of the Liberal Party has come to believe that they exist merely to hit restart on the Howard era. They appeared to think that Abbott's government was acting out some script from that Howard's first term (1996-98): first, confect a fiscal crisis for which the Opposition is, allegedly, solely to blame; second, announce any policy nasties and broken promises early on in the government's life; third, distract your opponents with a series of culture wars aimed at out-of-touch left-wing 'elites'; last, proceed triumphantly to the ballot box with the Howardista-mantra that 'you may not like us but we get the job done'. If only politics were so easy.

In the Liberals' imagination Howardism was hallmarked by its canny economic management and large budget surpluses, before its ideological overreach in implementing the unpopular industrial laws known as *WorkChoices*. As time goes on, however, the mythology surrounding Howard's electoral prowess is giving way to a more realistic story whereby his government did not discover some magical political elixir. Rather, it primarily benefited from fortunate economic conditions. Moreover, there is a growing realisation that our nation's most pressing public policy problems can be traced back to Howard's time in office, not to mention the genesis of lingering, destructive culture wars and debates over migration and national identity.

The Coalition are – or at least were – fond of talking up the need to tackle debt and deficit. It was a brutally effective rhetorical tactic during the Rudd-Gillard years, yet now hangs like an albatross after six years of Coalition deficits – deficits that have more than doubled the national debt without a GFC or recession to tackle or any major nation-building project to show for it. For this too it can largely thank Howard and his Treasurer Peter Costello's fiscal policy. It was Howard, in particular his government's final budget's tax (reducing personal rates) and expenditure (expanding middle-class welfare) policies, which locked in a structural deficit, an intergenerational malaise exposed by the GFC and the tapering off of a once-in-a-century mining boom. The mining boom-led also had the effect of concealing the downturn in productivity growth during the Howard years. Productive infrastructure investment was - and remains - grossly inadequate, whether road and rail transport, broadband internet, and other critical fields such as health, education, energy and more besides. Then we have the legacy of what unionist Misha Zelinsky calls Howard's 'Twin Gorillas' – negative gearing and capital gains tax deductions – that made Australia's housing market severely unaffordable.

Outside of economic policy, many Coalition MPs seek to replicate the imagined success of Howard's culture wars against so-called left-wing 'elites', for instance pushing for changes to section 18C of the *Racial Discrimination Act*. 'If only we prosecute the culture wars the Labor base splits', so the culture war logic goes. It's faulty in two senses. Howard won four straight elections largely because of generally favourable economic conditions, not culture war sorties over Aboriginal affairs, political correctness, nor even the mileage he made out of events such as Tampa and September 11, advantageous as they each were. Second, Howard was elected twenty-three years ago. There is a large swathe of the adult voting population who have very little recollection of those events or Howard's era – if they were alive at all. Then there is the small matter of climate change action and energy policy. Howard was dragged kicking and screaming to support an Emissions Trading Scheme prior to the 2007 federal election. Henceforth his party became staunch opponents of any form of carbon pricing and is still lukewarm. Turnbull's attempt to legislate for a National Energy Guarantee led to his downfall. Yet even before that inaction, the Howard government did precious little to promote solar power and other renewable sources of energy, leaving Australia miles behind developed economies such as Germany.

There is little sign of Liberal revisionism of the Howard era on the horizon which bodes ill for party hopes of policy making reinvigoration. Maybe, just maybe, Scott Morrison is the next Howard, though it arguably speaks to the infantilisation of Australia's natural governing party and media that it thinks in such terms.

As we hail each arriving Messiah so, too, we wait Godot-like for the next 'big reform'. One more change of prime minister or government might do the trick. We are told, and tell ourselves, we need big nation-building reform, which we often do, like in the days when Keating floated the dollar, Hawke slashed tariffs and Howard taxed goods and services, but are not patient enough to wait out the necessarily long and difficult public debates that big (rare) reforms require. As Emily Millane puts it for *The Conversation*: "not nearly enough time is spent considering the reasons why those reforms were successful, and what constituted success. Big reforms are aberrations. It's easy to bemoan that big reforms are not being repeated. There are things history teaches us about the nature of policy change. Another is that change happens all the time, less perceptibly, over increments ... [and] many of those who lament the lack of reform have barrows to push, often because of their own vested interests."[71]

Has Australian become ungovernable? The answer is only yes if we are seeking some political utopia, a nirvana which has not and will not materialise from the messy thing we call democracy. Yet Australia has clearly become less governable owing to a range of factors, not the least of which is the growing expectations we place upon national leaders, even as national governments have less and less ability to pull economic levers. If we want to politicians to pursue a long game, then we need to have the patience to reward the brave and the self-awareness to understand that transformational change cannot be 'done' in days or months. We need to check our expectations. Ultimately, we as a polity deserve the governments we elect and the false Messiahs we have willed into national leadership. The 2019 election, no matter Morrison's claims to believe in 'miracles', did not bear witness to Australians electing a prime ministerial Messiah.

Expectations-wise, that might be a very good thing for the prime minister and very bad news for federal Labor. For its part, a jaded Australian public is desperate for a return to some semblance of normality: where sport, not politics, is front page of the newspapers, and prime ministers survive to see out a three-year term in office. Whatever Morrison's best intentions, his government finds itself operating in a climate in which many believe Australia has become ungovernable, its policy dilemmas intractable and subject to partisanship, and its major parties beset by internecine conflict. We also remain a small trading nation subject to the vagaries of the global economy. We can't be sure the prime ministerial revolving door has ceased spinning. Morrison's hold on power was ostensibly cemented when in December 2018 the federal parliamentary Liberal party amended its rules for spilling the leadership: a super-majority of 66 per cent of the party-room is required to remove an elected prime minister. Yet David Crowe warns: "The rules adjust the price of power, not the hunger for it."[72] The question remains: how did Morrison win against the odds, after everything, in spite of his party? How did Labor lose the seemingly unloseable election, after everything, in spite of itself?

3

ONLY ACADEMIC IN THE VILLAGE

Monash University, March 2012

'Nick … Bill Shorten', the voice at the other end of the phone briskly announces.

'Bullshit it is', I think to myself as I punch out words in my office. 'Damo's playing another fucking prank. Pretty good impression though, I'll pay him that'.

I don't utter those words, fortunately. *It is* Bill Shorten.

It's March 2012 and storm clouds have gathered over Julia Gillard's minority Labor government. Deposed PM Kevin Rudd is waging a relentless insurgency.

And the Minister for Workplace Relations wants to talk.

About what? We met, briefly, years ago. The conversation couldn't have lasted more than a minute. Might be one of the bolshie political commentaries I've written for *The Age* newspaper since returning from a job in Sydney a few months back. The last subtlety termed former prime minister Rudd a Labor rat. Labor should not countenance any switch back to Rudd from Gillard, I argued, or be seen to reward terrorism. Other options, such as drafting Shorten to the leadership, would burn a next generation Labor leader. I had followed his career closely as he climbed the ranks of the Australian Workers' Union, rebuilding the fallen giant of Australian labour, from organiser to Victorian branch secretary (1998) to national secretary (2001) and then entered federal parliament as the Labor member for Maribyrnong in the 2007 Ruddslide. I'd written about him in passing as one of Labor's rising stars.

Shorten seemed to get it. I was struck by his first speech in 2008, the leitmotiv of which concerned the good life. It read like a paean to my communitarian outlook. "How to achieve a long, meaningful life in a rapidly changing world", Shorten told federal parliament, "is one of the great themes of our new century ... I believe our institutions will have to rethink the way they do things ... What I want to accomplish for working people is about aspiration—not for material wealth and plasma televisions alone but for 100 years of health; for education and skills to do quality, interesting work; for living in decent and supportive communities; and for leading a rewarding and meaningful life.'[73] Shorten had drawn my attention somewhat earlier. In the aftermath of Labor's disastrous defeat at the 2004 federal election under Mark Latham, he penned a much reported upon essay for the Fabian Society. "The principal lesson from four federal election losses is clear: Labor has failed to establish its economic management credentials to voters in the provincial centres and outer suburbs of metropolitan Australia. In an economy driven by record levels of personal, household and private sector debt, interest rates and economic management are the top vote-changing issues", Shorten diagnosed, correctly. "Economic credibility is a gateway through which Labor must pass before it can bring its policy strengths in health and education to bear. In 2004, Labor failed to dent the Coalition's commanding lead as economic managers. Instead, Labor relied on its traditional strengths in health care and education, together with a dramatic appeal in environment policy. Historically, the ALP has performed best by being the party of big economic ideas that give confidence to all Australians. Labor's task now is to move to the Centre." For good measure, Shorten identified one of the key factors holding Labor back – its prioritisation of progressive issues over mainstream concerns.

The big 'L' Left appeals meant that Federal Labor vacated the centre ground for Howard to exploit. In this era of 'conservative populism', the traditional understanding of left-right political discourse is an oversimplification of the Australian electorate. There is also a 'top-down' divide, between highly educated, urban intelligentsia (who, despite Party differences, share similar liberal social values and an economically rationalist acceptance of globalisation) and so-called 'ordinary Australians' in the suburbs and regions (who are risk-averse to economic restructuring and suspicious of liberal social values). Howard has retained his conservative supporters in the Right intelligentsia, while gaining newer supporters in 'Middle Australia' through his 'dog-whistle' rhetoric about issues such as border security, gay marriage and the US alliance. By contrast, Labor's support has been increasingly confined to the Left intelligentsia with its post-Whitlam emphasis on progressive policies on the environment, refugees and multiculturalism. The policy priorities of the Left are not wrong, but they have acquired a prominence that is now a barrier to Labor reconnecting with both its blue-collar base and middle Australia. The issues of greatest concern to the Left must become less prominent in Labor campaigning.[74]

Shorten wasted no time on the backbench. As Rudd's parliamentary secretary for disabilities and children's services – his absence from cabinet was regarded as something of a slight – he put the National Disability Insurance Scheme on the nation's agenda, using the skills acquired as a union organiser to gather together disparate disability interest groups. Shorten revelled in the role – truth be told he was too wet behind the ears to automatically enter cabinet. He *organised* – getting people in the same room, listening to people's stories, plucking their smartest ideas, and putting their case within the government and in the media. Shorten was not interested in generating tears for disabled Australians. He was organising to win.

***

Bill and I talk intensely above the hubbub of a mostly student patronised cafe. It's mostly me talking, really. Shorten is a listener. Sure, he disarms and flatters, and likes to be flattered – I tell him I think he has the makings of a "fine Labor prime minister". Shorten is more charismatic than his public persona lets on; for some reason it doesn't translate to the screen. Part of this is Shorten's innate caution. Another explanation, I discover, is the role played by the advisor class and politicians themselves. In their fruitless quest to avoid gotcha moments and public faux pas, politicians have allowed themselves to be coached into daleks, as the former Victorian Labor powerbroker Robert Ray memorably described their evolution. Tactics are valued over strategy, even when one's interests are best served by appearing human; that is, to err.

Shorten is thinking about the long game. He is looking beyond the horizon of the 2013 election – one which Labor is almost certain to lose. He soaks up information like a sponge. Names. Statistics. Mutual friends. Knows his history. He's looking for answers – challenging points of view, a way through this mess. Even, it appears, from an over-opinionated lecturer. I'm schooled myself. Politicians want answers, quickly. There is no time in this world for seminar-room reflection, though they might surely benefit from more of that – Whitlam, Hawke and Keating all understood its value.

Bill asks me what I think the problem with modern Labor is, to which I respond, to the best of my memory:

> "They don't like us. The electorate that is. Working-class people. Don't trust us. Haven't trusted us since the early 1990s recession. "The recession we had to have"? Give me a break. No one needed a recession. Keating ought to have apologised for that line. Rudd, Gillard, they are a symptom rather than cause of this mess. People never forgave us: millions of voters who voted Labor all their lives. Don't forget their kids. They saw their Dads and Mums, and parents of friends lose their

jobs, they saw the factories, almost whole industries close. Savings evaporate. Houses foreclosed on. Sure, they accepted some matters were beyond our control, but 'had to have?"

Shorten seems momentarily startled. Is this the first time he's heard such an interpretation? Maybe it's the source. The Labor Left and anti-Labor Left have long viewed with suspicion – if not hostility – the market reforms of the Hawke-Keating era. They only took a shine to 'Keating, prime minister' on social and cultural issues. Mabo and Reconciliation. The Republic. Multiculturalism. Our place in Asia. But this view is coming from someone associated with the Right. Keating was of the NSW Right too and his success, first as treasurer, then as the PM who won the unwinnable 1993 election, testifies to the influence the Right wielded in the 1980s and 90s.

Paul Keating inspired me to love politics, to live politics. It was tribal Keating – those flamboyant, visceral attacks on the Tories in question time – which led me to join the Australian Labor Party as a nineteen-year-old university student, just as Shorten had been pulled into the party's orbit by Hawke's prime ministership a decade earlier. I'd followed Hawke and Keating with an unusual passion as a teenager, even as a transfixed child glued to the television, waiting for the news to finish. It's an odd feeling, then, to lecture one of the great man's successors and possible prime minister on his failings. Keatingism is part of Labor's problem, not the solution. Bill listens, I catch a nod here and there. Consternation at points. He keeps listening.

'Return to the lessons of the Hawke-Keating government' we have been told ad infinitum since the party lost power in a landslide at the 1996 federal election. For my part I've determined that if this is Labor Gen X's best game, and Bill and I are both members of this club albeit a decade apart, then it's time to give up, give back the keys to the car to Bob and Paul or pass on the leadership baton to someone else. It's time to strike out on our own; creating a legacy which future generations will aspire to emulate. I was five when Hawke won office and legally able – just – to buy alcohol when Keating lost power; Bill was respectively sixteen and on the cusp of his thirties. Those Labor governments spanned my entire childhood. They changed Australia forever and for the better. But I'm in my mid-30s (now early-40s), a university lecturer, a father and author; Bill's a decade older and a cabinet minister. It's time, alright. My friend Michael Cooney put it perfectly a few years later. "If we really believe we are just Bob and Paul's dumb-arse step-kids, we should pack up and go home."[75]

I come away from meeting Bill Shorten wanting to work for the bloke. We are different, the two of us. I'm not a natural politician despite throwing my hat into the ring of a Labor preselection six years later (unsuccessfully as it happened ... perhaps proving my own point). I'm prone to existential angst and self-doubt – some friends, politely and impolitely, say I live up to the stereotype of the neurotic Jew. Bill is most definitely a politician, a born-to-be politician if ever there was one. He's resilient. He is, as another academic Geoff Robinson has written, unlike intellectuals – being "unencumbered by doubt, whereas the certainty of Kevin Rudd and Tony Abbott obscured a private uncertainty ... He is undaunted by knockbacks and disappointments."[76] Unlike Rudd he is tribal Labor. There are no doubts to his pedigree, no matter factional faultlines. No one in Labor asks: 'Is Bill one of us?'

Yet I see something of his story and that of his family's reflected in my own. We are both sons of driven, feminist (without claiming to be feminist) working-class Ballarat women who went to the University of Melbourne on teacher's scholarships and became first-class schoolteachers and more. It's a point his wife Chloe quickly discerns. Bill is hyper-ambitious – more ambitious than I could ever imagine – but firmly rooted within the Labor tradition; he has an instinctive feel for the party, its tribalism, its quirks, its idiosyncrasies. Neither of us really chose the party. It chose us. The same with unionism. It makes us old-fashioned in a professional political world where both major parties attract MPs and staffers who could easily be a member of their rival. Shorten can imagine himself as PM, which might be the half the trick of convincing others. He convinced me. In 2012 I felt he was destined to become PM.

I'm not certain he gets a grasp on me, however. 'Dr Nick', as he calls me, isn't easy to pin down. I'm not like other academics, that's for sure. A bit rough around the edges. I'm different from the staffer class too – for a start I've had a career outside of the party. I'm a bit like the late blooming footy player who jumps off the rookie list in their mid20s – only I enter the fray in my mid-30s. I'm perhaps naïve, having avoided Young Labor like the plague after a visit to one state conference. Politics, I discover, slowly and painfully, has the potential to encourage ordinarily decent people to act in the most dreadful manner to one another. Friends and allies will lie to your face. They will betray you without blinking. Some of the hypocrisy is breathtaking. Labor is a party committed to decent, fair treatment in the workplace. Yet if its treatment of some staff and MPs were held up to the same standards as the rest of the workplace, the party would have been put out of business eons ago. Self-identifying feminists will fulminate against the patriarchy and yet in actually existing cases where a male and female employee have entered into a consensual relationship, the fracture of that relationship has seen the woman punted. Gender solidarity be damned.

Ideologically, I confound. 'Communist' and 'shocking right-winger' are epithets thrown my way by Bill, each delivered with a boyish grin, and only half-jokingly. I enjoy confounding the man who can read most rooms he walks into and most people he meets. Bill and I agree to keep in touch. By year's end we are talking about a job in his ministerial office. A year to the date of our first meeting I'm on Team Shorten.

The only academic in the village.

***

Whether God votes Tory or is a bleeding heart with a cruel sense of humour, Labor has been fated to take national office in the shadows of calamity. In 1914 Fisher became Labor prime minister for the third time in the first months of the Great War. He lasted a little over a year. Labor subsequently 'blew out its brains' and split over the issue of conscription in late 1916. When Jim Scullin returned the party to the treasury benches after more than a decade in the political wilderness his government was torn apart by the effects of the early 1930s Great Depression. John Curtin and Gough Whitlam respectively took office in periods of global war and economic downturn.

So it was that in 2008 Labor was confronted by the onset of the Global Financial Crisis (GFC). Whereas during the Great Depression Jim Scullin's government imploded and then was routed at the ballot box, spearheaded by Prime Minister and Treasurer, Rudd and Swan, Labor assembled a successful, multi-stage $75 billion economic stimulus package and implemented measures to shore up the banking system. Aided by continuing Chinese demand for natural resources, alone among the advanced economies Australia avoided recession; unemployment peaked at less than six per cent. Granted, the burden still fell on working people: many were forced to accept part-time work or put wage claims on hold. And Labor would eventually fall victim to its own success. As former Labor minister Neal Blewett observed at the time, "When recession was avoided, the population had little sense of the danger averted".[77] Following Tony Abbott's ascension to the Liberal leadership and the failure of the Copenhagen Conference on climate change to reach agreement – both events taking place in late 2009 – the government began to falter. Legislation to introduce an emissions trading scheme was abandoned in early 2010 having been twice blocked in the

Senate, including by the Greens. Controversy raged over the administration and size of the Rudd government's stimulus package. Public concern about 'illegal immigration' saw the government suspend applications by Afghan and Sri Lankan refugees. Finally, a proposed Resource Super Profits Tax sparked an ugly brawl between the battling government and the giant mining companies.

In the Age of Twitter, events moved quickly. In the space of twenty-four hours, seemingly idle media gossip turned into speculation that Rudd's leadership was terminal. I vividly recall the shock of seeing my mate Paul Howes, then AWU National Secretary, going on the ABC's *Lateline* to pronounce the deed was done. The next morning, on 24 June 2010, an emotional Rudd stepped down as prime minister. Gillard, aged forty-eight, became Australia's twenty-seventh – and first female – prime minister. Shorten was promoted into the Labor ministry as Assistant Treasurer and Minister for Financial Services and Superannuation, before entering Cabinet proper in 2011 as Workplace Relations Minister. Following Gillard's snap announcement of an August election, during which she was bedevilled by damaging leaks emanating from Rudd or his supporters, the Labor government was returned in September 2010, dependent for its survival on a motley alliance of Greens politicians and rural independents. The vexed issues of asylum-seekers and budget deficit continued to weigh on Labor, even if Gillard's government was productive in a legislative sense. Rudd launched an unsuccessful attempt to wrest back the prime ministership in February 2012. But Rudd won't give up; psychologically he couldn't give up.

A year later I decided to accept a job offer from Shorten – a front seat to the last days of Rome. I loved the job. I'd never written a speech for anyone else before in my life – it's a steep learning curve and more anxiety inducing than writing anything in my own name. Someone else's reputation is on the line. My first effort is a stinker, but a necessary experience. I learn a lot from

Joel Deane, poet, author and former speechwriter to Victorian Labor premiers Steve Bracks and John Brumby. He is incredibly kind, patient and generous – and recovering from a stroke. Speechwriting is a confidence game – my second attempt is better, the third for the National Press Club better again. The legendary Labor speechwriter and playwright Bob Ellis, who watched it on television, emails to say as much: he's 'jealous'. Bob Ellis is 'jealous'. I'm enjoying the gig – it's addictive – perhaps because I know it has a short shelf-life.

Rudd launched a second, this time successful, challenge to Gillard's leadership on 26 June 2013. Shorten, now a senior Cabinet minister, publicly announced his switch of support, pleading Labor's electoral survival. It was a decision which strained him – I witnessed its toll up close – a strain obvious to anyone watching his press conference backing Rudd. Later that night we debriefed over beers in the office. He seemed calm, the boyish grin reappearing as he ribbed me over what might happen to the history of the AWU I was writing. Shorten's judgement would, in the short-term, prove justified, but Rudd could not save Labor. And while Shorten energetically made the case for Labor in his new portfolio of education, I fretted about the damage done to his leadership prospects. Would this be an albatross around Shorten's neck?

It is true that Shorten took too long to untangle himself from factional wheeling and dealing. He almost certainly underplayed his role in the first coup, while his role in the latter is grossly overstated. Then again, I had begun to detect a trend within the party and the Canberra gallery: underestimating Shorten. Some of it is class snobbery or anti-Labor bias, some of it jealously. He wouldn't make it as a unionist, they said. Yet age 31 he became the Victorian head of the AWU in 1998, and national secretary three years later. He went onto win preselection and a seat in parliament and was a more than effective parliamentary secretary and minister, spearheading the NDIS. He'd keep confounding the naysayers. It's all academic for the time being. After proceeding to the polls with indecent haste, Rudd's second Labor government was swept from office at the September 2013 election losing by a seventeen-seat margin on a nationwide 3.6 per cent two party swing. Shorten suffered a six per cent swing in his own seat.

The dust had barely settled on the 2013 campaign when another began in earnest. Under new rules for electing and deselecting leaders, rank-and-file members played a role in the process following Rudd's resignation as Labor leader on election night. An equal 50 per cent weighting of caucus and party member votes served as the new basis of electing the leader, along the lines of the model once used by British Labour in 2010 for the election of party leader. (The UK model has since changed, with zero weighting for MPs in the party's leadership process, a factor that keeps Corbyn in power.) Would Shorten run? I was convinced he had to and made the case. Sure, he needed more time and he was staring at a large government majority and at best five to six years of opposition, but there is rarely a perfect time to run. If NSW left-winger Anthony Albanese – known universally as Albo – ran uncontested there was no chance of recovering the leadership. Shorten, not to mention a future leadership contender from the Right, would find it impossible to win a rank-and-file ballot again. Plus, I had done the maths – if he could secure the ballots of enough caucus votes he could win. And I thought he could win. Fortunately, enough heavy hitters aligned with my judgment – Bill Kelty and Steve Conroy perhaps the most notable, even if the latter was ropeable and, rightly so, at the shambolic Rudd rules. Little did commentators know they were unconstitutional as the parliamentary party cannot dictate party rules to the ALP's highest decision-making forum, national conference, which it effectively did. This was later amended by conference, but it would have taken a single complaint for the entire process to have been invalidated. More than just a startling oversight by a highly-professional organisation, the changes proved again how Rudd's authoritarian approach was inherently at odds with Labor's collectivist democratic traditions.

Bill thrived during the campaign, which we modelled on Gough Whitlam's 1967 promise of 'Party. Policy. People'. "This year the party; next year the policy; 1969 the people."[78] Of course, we didn't have three years. Over the next month no stone was left unturned, no conversation not had, and no vote not sought as Bill travelled the length and breadth of the continent. Team Shorten, and the Right generally, were immensely disciplined, notwithstanding the errorism of one staffer who decided to insert a commitment to exploring LGBTQ quotas in Bill's manifesto. While Bill didn't win a majority of rank and file votes, he won more than many thought possible, particularly given the poor performance in Queensland, and as I saw close up in debating forums he won the respect of party members who surely did not vote for him. My sense, too, was that the Albo forces were complacent. Where we compiled a glossy publication spruiking Bill's leadership quality, policy ideas and vision for the party, the other mob circulated what looked like a cheap branch newsletter. After a polite yet energetic contest, Bill won the Labor leadership on 10 October 2013.

Bill was now one step, although a large step, from his goal of the Lodge.

For my part I departed the office. With the birth of my second child and three books to write, I didn't feel like I could give 100 per cent to the job, one demanding working days of eighteen hours and time away from family. I'd regret my choice.

Despite the new rules ostensibly insulating the leader from a challenge many didn't believe he would see out the term – if it wasn't Albo, then a next generation leader from NSW might knock him off. Yet Shorten assiduously managed his intra-party relationships. The Rudd rules helped, serving to inoculate Shorten's leadership from any quick and decisive challenge in times of polling strife and external political pressure. Yet they counted for little if relations between leader and party in all its facets, factions and forceful personalities were mismanaged. This dynamic tension translated into policy: as leader Shorten campaigned on a program of unashamed Labor pedigree – wages and penalty rates, health, education and housing affordability, railed against big business tax cuts, and argued for redistributive reforms in superannuation, capital gains and negative gearing. Inequality and fairness – though I felt the vagueness of the latter term was problematic – were placed at the centre of Labor's offering. Shorten more than most recognised that the market liberalisation orthodoxy of three decades had exhausted its economic and political utility. He embraced a more activist role for government, even, as a figure from the Right, taking the party left at a time when popular sentiment was pointing in that direction, which also served the purpose of mollifying left-of-centre critics within the party.

Shorten proved adept at identifying opponents' weaknesses and focussing his energies at the weakest point, a lesson gleaned from his love of military strategy. Abbott, he surmised, was too right-wing and too macho for the populace, notwithstanding his election victory; and he quickly identified as his target the prime minister's pursuit of an unmandated agenda lacking fairness. Shorten's leadership was certainly aided by Abbott's follies. Episodes such as the 2014 budget debacle – which backflipped on core election promises not to cut funding to health, education and more besides – were a once-in-a-generation political gift and gratefully accepted as such by Shorten and his shadow treasurer Chris Bowen.[79] Yet the attack on the budget's unfairness was carried without the aggressive incivility that characterised Abbott's tenure as opposition leader. Ideological flights of fancy such as appointing a 'freedom commissioner' to the Human Rights Commission and the failed repeal of section 18c of the *Racial Discrimination Act*, knighting Prince Philip and Bronwyn Bishop's "Choppergate" made Abbott a once-in-a-generation laughing stock. Even a royal commission into union corruption – designed to damage Shorten – backfired after the commissioner, Dyson Heydon, accepted an invitation to speak at a Liberal Party fundraiser.

Shorten's leadership seemed made for the times in other ways. "Unpretentious in performance, he largely succeeded in binding Labor's wounds from the Rudd-Gillard era", noted Paul Strangio in his review of Bill's 2016 book, *For the Common Good*:

> He has nestled into the bosom of the party following the familial traumas catalysed by the reign of the imperious Kevin Rudd ... Throughout Labor's history there has been a spectrum of leaders ranging from those who have worked with the grain of the party's power-sharing principles (group leaders) and those who have chafed against them (personalisers). Outliers of the latter category include ... Billy Hughes and, more recently, Rudd. Brilliant and creative spirits, but wilful and controlling, they have had a convulsive effect on the party. In turn, the party's response to being burnt by excessive personalising leadership has been to retreat into a period of closing ranks and recuperation under a group leader. Enter Shorten.[80]

Abbott's prime ministership had been fatally weakened by the February 2015 leadership ballot in which he stood successfully against an 'empty chair'. Citing the loss of thirty Newspolls in a row, Turnbull struck seven months later. On 14 September 2015, in a vote for the Liberal leadership, Abbott was defeated by Turnbull, who became Prime Minister the following day. Turnbull's coup against Abbott raised expectations that a more 'progressive' prime minister would move the Coalition closer to the centre of Australian politics. Such hopes were dashed: a refreshed Coalition agreement strengthened the National Party's hand. The scale of Turnbull's indebtedness to his party's Right had not yet been revealed; nor had Tony Abbott's final broken promise as prime minister of 'no sniping' been fully realised.

"You told me to run", Bill half-jokingly scolds me when we speak in mid-2015. "Don't worry too much about Turnbull", I reassure him. "He's a dud, won't last." At least he takes my call. I'd written a critical piece for *The Monthly* a few months back arguing that not talking debt and deficits and vacating the hard-economic space in favour of an all-encompassing language of fairness was a recipe for trouble. I'd singled out Bill for criticism – he was sleep walking to electoral defeat.[81] Bill wasn't happy and let me know. While he may not have appreciated the public dressing down, Shorten was in strife at the end of 2015. Some Laborites were descending into insanity – thinking about changing leaders again, hoping for a different outcome.

While his enemies counted, Shorten had identified Turnbull's fatal weaknesses – he was fighting a war on two fronts, material and idealistic. Here was a millionaire prime minister ruling during a time of economic anxiety – all the while spouting slogans about 'exciting times' and 'agility', terms most people identify with job losses and pay cuts. And here was a 'progressive' Liberal leader – one who had sought Labor preselection years ago – unwilling and seemingly unable to rule on his own terms. It was dawning on others that Turnbull wasn't much good at this politics thing after all. Changes were also made to Shorten's office – my return easily the most marginal. Most significant was the recruitment of Cameron Milner, former Queensland Labor state secretary and experienced campaigner. Shorten's trusted media advisor, former Swan staffer Ryan Liddell, became de facto deputy chief – he would in time assume the head role in 2017 – along with fellow-traveller, economist Amit Singh. Shorten's media appearances improved. Zingers fell by the wayside. He was running a lot, daily, which is good for the waistline and the mind. Milner also got Shorten match fit for the campaign to come by honing his presentation skills in so-called town hall appearances, and in regular interviews, doorstops, sitting days and speeches. He had if anything become more resilient after the hits he had taken over the preceding two years – false rape allegations, the royal commission and his mother Ann's sudden death. Fatherhood and Chloe had changed Shorten too – it made him a better leader; it gave a real-world edge to having empathy for those much mythologised working families. Yet Shorten entered the 2016 election campaign once more underestimated. Most thought the best that could be achieved was a result which put Labor back within striking distance. Winning twenty-one seats from a first-term government was a mountain too great to climb. Clawing back between ten to twelve seats is regarded as a pass mark, though no one is sure if that would hold off his rival Anthony Albanese from challenging for the leadership as the federal party's rules mandated.

Shorten, Australian voters, and eventually Turnbull's colleagues, had other ideas. Labor's performance exceeded expectations. The Coalition government nearly lost office at the 2 July federal election, a two-month-long marathon affair – playing to Shorten's strengths and his comparative youth vis-à-vis a weary Turnbull – which featured nary a word on the key legislative subject that Turnbull used to trigger the ballot: workplace relations. Labor came within one seat of knocking off a first-term government, even if its House of Representatives' primary vote of 34.73 per cent remained unhealthily low. The Turnbull government's majority was reduced to a single seat – Labor won a net total of fourteen seats. The 2016 election loss, albeit narrow, gave Shorten three things: further campaign experience; more confidence, both in himself and in the party's campaign machine; and a lifeline to remain leader for another term. Bill had survived. He knew he had Turnbull's measure.

Shorten convinced enough colleagues to renew his leadership. It was no guarantee of avoiding the fate of Bill Hayden and Kim Beazley, however – Labor leaders who delivered first-up honourable election losses, but never grasped the prize of the prime ministership. Yet Shorten was far more ruthless than either man, as I was to discover from personal experience.

While I struggled to admit it at the time, the breakdown of my marriage during my second coming in the Opposition Leader's office had taken a toll, if that adequately describes the loss of my best friend. People often described a feeling of brokenness and it sounds like a cliché, but that's how it felt, not that there was much sympathy in an office of mainly twenty-somethings. It's also an office which had changed for the worse, though I'm scarcely an impartial observer. It's younger; few staff have families or partners; of the political staffers I'm either the third or fourth oldest at 38. It's more 'progressive'. And it's lacking diversity of opinion. There are genuine stars around – I don't think I've ever seen a harder-working, sharper staffer than the South Australian Andrew Anson. Milner is a genuine leader – huge work-ethic, strategic and always calm. It's a great shame he looks unlikely to go into parliament himself. However, much of the old guard from the Rudd-Gillard years has coalesced in Bill's and other offices determined to protect the legacy of those years. And while there are operators adept at playing ruthless office politics, take-no-prisoners political advice is less forthcoming. Bill is somewhat empathetic to my situation, but not prepared to challenge the status quo. As Shorten proceeded on a post-election 'victory lap' around the nation, I nursed a bruised ego, wounded heart and several hangovers on a newly single man's holiday to Israel. So much for the Promised Land. I spend days – is it weeks? – staring forlornly into the glistening Mediterranean on Tel Aviv's Banana Beach, playing the iconic 1980s Aussie pop-rock-group Icehouse's *Electric Blue* on repeat. I begin writing this book.

***

The 2016 election result – and Turnbull's further loss of authority – eliminated any possibility of a more centrist Coalition. The government was rocked by successive controversies: Barnaby Joyce's own marital woes and MPs running foul of Section 44 of the constitution. Abbott continued to destabilise the government. All the while, many Australians were treading water. Real wages growth was at record lows. Job creation bent towards part-time and casual employment. The spectre of a new recession hovered. On 21 August 2018, Turnbull spectacularly spilled the Liberal leadership, surviving the resultant challenge by conservative poster boy and Home Affairs Minister, Queenslander Peter Dutton, 48 votes to 35. The challenge had in the manner of Abbott's fall, fatally weakened Turnbull, and brought to the surface intractable ideological tensions between moderate Liberals led by Turnbull, and conservative warriors such as Dutton and Abbott. The party voted in favour of holding a second ballot a few days later; Turnbull chose not to be a candidate. In the second vote, Treasurer Scott Morrison emerged as a compromise candidate, defeating Dutton and Julie Bishop to become leader of the Liberal Party and prime minister. In his final press conference as Prime Minister, Turnbull helpfully denounced Dutton and Abbott as "wreckers". Shorten had seen off two prime ministers, yet in Morrison faced a more instinctive political animal, a Liberal tribalist, who immediately went on an election footing, even if it would take over seven months for the new prime minister to call a ballot, one announced shortly after a moderately well-received budget.

Five and a half years in Opposition steeled Bill Shorten. He was arguably the most effective Labor Opposition Leader since Whitlam. He rebuilt a shell-shocked party, brought down two prime ministers, and crafted a policy mandate for government, if he could win. Yet, now, for perhaps the first time in his career, Shorten found himself the favourite and not to be underestimated. Me? I was to be found in the cheap seats, a chronicler, rather than a participant in the making of Australian history.

4

CHEAP SEATS

Day 1: Oggy and the cockroaches

Children are the ultimate lesson in humility. It's 8am on Thursday April 11: Prime Minister Scott Morrison has just called the 2019 federal election. Polling day is set for 18 May. Labor needs to win a net four seats to form government and Bill Shorten will realise his aim of becoming Prime Minister. Labor will be back in power five and a half years after the crushing defeat of 2013. I'm frantically scouring the news, catching a glimpse of the leader's opening gambits. My two children are blissfully unaware of a national ballot which will shape their futures and possibly the future of their kids. It's all about Weetbix, Sultana Bran and their favourite TV series of the moment, a quirky French cartoon, 'Oggy and the cockroaches'. Oggy, an anthropomorphic cat, spends his days watching television and eating: that's if he isn't being pestered by three roaches, Joey, Dee Dee and Marky, named after members of *The Ramones*. There's no dialogue. It's not a bad metaphor for the election – cockroaches, like politicians, are ubiquitous and notoriously difficult to kill off – and to add to the reference, Oggy shares his name with the partner of the Greens candidate in my local seat.

Morrison kicks off the election in Canberra speaking from the prime minister's courtyard in Parliament House, projecting all the authority of the office. He is sharp and energetic. He puts the economy front and centre and invokes the spectre of his political inspiration, John Howard. "We live in the best country in the world," he announces. "But to secure your future, the road ahead depends on a strong economy. And that's why there is so much at stake at this election". He consciously draws upon Howard's 2004 election 'trust' pitch, asking "who do you trust to deliver that strong economy which your essential services rely on?"[82]

The trust line reminds me of what I'm missing out on. I once wrote an election-time speech for Shorten on the same theme: 'who do you trust' with your children's education. Got a great run in the media and annoyed the Coalition. I drop my kids at their holiday program and rush to the office. I'm glued to the phone in between meetings and my son's footy training. I've perhaps un- wisely volunteered as the under 9's team manager, a more com- plicated gig than I expected. Why am I so manic? I'm not cam- paigning. 'Sent to Coventry', I joke to colleagues. I console myself that it's no biggie. I've got a lot on my plate. I and my new partner are expecting – my third child – and I'm writing this book. Who am I kidding? It hurts sitting here in the cheap seats away from the real action, proximate to power and influence, even if all I can offer are words. As Labor speechwriter Don Watson memorably wrote in his memoir of Keating's prime ministership: 'The body keeps twitching after the head is cut off'.[83]

None of what occurs in the PM's courtyard or on day one, two or in the next five weeks changes the basic arithmetic: Labor needs to win four net seats. The government is already behind – after byelections and redistributions in Victoria, the ACT and South Australia, Labor has a notional 72 of the House of Representatives' 151 seats versus the Coalition's 73. Morrison remains behind in the polls, where the government has been for most of the past three years. 52 Newspolls in a row. The Coalition has not won any of the 153 opinion polls carried out by an established pollster since September 2016. Everything points to a Labor victory. 52.5 per cent to 47.5 per cent is the average two-party polling, which would give Labor a comfortable majority, but not a landslide – it never works that way for federal Labor, not with Rudd in 2007 or Hawke in 1983 or Whitlam's 1972 triumph. Queensland is a worry, or parts thereof, so too Western Australia, perhaps Tasmania. Victoria is a key battleground state; Labor hopes to repeat the Andrews Labor government's thumping win in late 2018. If Shorten loses, the reckoning inside Labor will be momentous.

It all comes down to risk. If enough Australians, in enough seats, judge that there's a risk in voting Labor, they will stick with the devil they know, despite the Coalition's chronic leadership instability, and despite the government's policy torpor. Morrison is hammering this angle. Shorten is painted as a risk to economic growth and budget surpluses which, after all, pay for health and education. He is presented as the embodiment of the Coalition's claim that Labor 'can't manage money'. "So it is crystal clear, at this election, it is a choice between me as prime minister and Bill Shorten as prime minister. You vote for me, you'll get me. You vote for Bill Shorten and you'll get Bill Shorten," he announces, to some mockery in the media. They mocked John Howard, too, mocked all the way to four election victories on a trot. Morrison's line is also a counter to the 'Team Labor' mantra promulgated by the Opposition. The strategy is to personalise the choice, to make the contest presidential. Labor people also forget that the turbulent 2007-13 era isn't that long ago – Morrison is hellbent on reminding voters. "The last time Labor was elected to form a government back in 2007 they inherited a strong economy and they inherited budget surpluses, and in the space of one year they turned a $20bn surplus into a $27bn deficit. They turned strong borders into weak borders, and we have spent the last more than 10 years getting back to where we were. You vote Labor once, you pay for it for a decade." It's not a bad line, though Morrison is no Howard, he doesn't have the deep experience of incumbency, nor the roaring economy enjoyed by the leader he is channelling. And he is asking voters to forget too, namely the unedifying spectacle of three Liberal prime ministers in five and a half years, and of course to forget the small matter of the GFC which confronted Labor in office.

Shorten starts in a backyard in the Melbourne suburb of Mitcham in the seat of Deakin, once regarded as safe for the Liberals but now winnable for Labor, post-Turnbull. It's interpreted as a sign of Shorten's confidence as the campaign begins and contrasts sharply with Morrison's Canberra launchpad. Shorten talks of giving punters a "fair go" without the division of the Coalition over the past six years. "If you are dissatisfied with the last six years, if you want better than the last six years, if you want a fair go for all Australians, if you want a government who is united and not constantly trying to tear each other down, then vote Labor on May 18."[84] The "case to vote Labor", Shorten says, is founded on its plans to deliver more jobs, higher pay, better health and education outcomes, as well as action on climate change and eco-friendly measures to drive energy prices down. This is what they call the 'grid' of issues – I've never quite worked out why key policies need to have a nickname – and we'll hear its key themes repeated ad infinitum over the next thirty-eight days. "We'll get on top of cost of living burdens and we'll get wages moving again in this country". "We can manage the economy in the interests of working and middle class people."

It's solid Labor stuff, the calculated risk I urged upon Bill and co. after 2013 – an ambitious, big-hearted social democratic agenda, a reworking of the economy on Labor's favoured ground of fairness, an agenda properly costed, and an agenda framed, Rudd-like, as a contest between Labor as the party of the 'future' versus a government 'stuck in the past'. Yet I shift uneasily. Labor activists and twitterati mocked me and others for focussing on economic management and issues such as mounting government debt over the past five and a half years. 'Neo-liberal!', they scoffed. Yet broad-brush economics cannot be avoided during the heat of an election when meta-narratives over spending and costings dominate. Most peacetime federal elections are a referendum on the economy; neither side can afford to vacate the field. Debt matters to working class people. And Morrison has enough political rat cunning not to repeat the follies of Turnbull. He will go negative and stay negative. This campaign is relatively short, certainly compared with 2016 which favoured the younger, campaign-fit Shorten over the less ruthless Turnbull. Labor's policies will now be assessed and scare mongered over as a genuine governing alternative, again unlike 2016.

Labor is vulnerable on climate change again, especially as it has recently made a big deal over electric vehicles. The party has set an ambitious policy target of 50 per cent of new sales of EVs by 2030 and the entire government car fleet by 2025. Here Morrison lands a few punches but goes over the top in accusing Shorten of wanting to "end the weekend".[85] Nonetheless: will people buy EVs, are they affordable and reliable? Where will we charge them and for how long? Will they generate a local industry and well-paying jobs? It seems to me that if Labor can't answer those questions the policy is dead on arrival. It's talking to Greens' voters, post-material types. They probably won't vote Labor and are not the sort of median voter Labor needs to win Deakin.

Morrison is no Howard, I reassure myself. This isn't the old man versus Latham. And it's not all about the leader – you've written most of a book on the subject. Labor's ground game is stronger, as, ostensibly, is that of the unionists out in the field, although our messaging on the latter score began to trouble me. The fundamentals haven't changed. Voters don't need to look at numbers to feel harried in economic terms. Today, my colleague Frank Bongiorno makes the point that this is really Australia's first post-GFC election, given the economy's earlier resilience.[86] Growth remains weak. People are concerned about stagnant wages – or for that matter finding and holding onto a job – and living standards. This is 1972 redux: a bumbling, backward-looking Coalition team with an uninspiring leader and recent history of leadership changes, up against a reform-minded Labor opposition. Sure, Shorten is no Whitlam, but the parallels are clear: leaders who won sizeable swings with first up efforts in 1969 and 2016, setting up realistic tilts at office three years later.

Just before bed, news breaks that Julian Assange has belatedly departed the Ecuadorian embassy in London. He is promptly arrested by British authorities for breaking bail. Soon circulating are YouTube parodies of Assange set to the cult audio of an Australian man, Charles Dosza, arrested over dodging a bill for a 'succulent Chinese meal.' I dream of Oggy and Bill that night. What a time to be asleep.

Week One: The Bill Australia Can't Afford

A good mate likes to claim credit for the saying: 'No plan survives first contact with the enemy'. Morrison is firing bullets, scattergun-like, seeking to unnerve Shorten. As the PM hot foots it to the hallowed electoral ground of Western Sydney, the Coalition open fire on the election's first full day by releasing what it calls Treasury estimates projecting Labor would raise $387 billion over 10 years via its "tax hits on the economy."[87] Labor seems flat-footed. It's odd given that the party has spent much of its time in Opposition focussed on taxation – promising to shut loopholes and eschew long-term, expensive income tax cuts in favour of higher surpluses, lower debt and better services. Here, the smart, usually ultra-disciplined, Chris Bowen, gift wraps the Coalition an attack line, in Keatingesque terms telling an interviewer in reference to retirees: "If they feel that this is something that should impact on their vote they are, of course, perfectly entitled to vote against us". I'm yet to see any TV adverts. Labor's campaign video – restricted to Twitter and Facebook – strikes me as slightly weird, possibly because I know Bill, and it's always odd to see yourself or people you know on the screen. Introducing himself, Shorten for a moment sounds like Lawrence Mooney, the comedian best known for impersonating then PM Malcolm Turnbull.

On the Friday morning news there is footage of a billboard of Shorten's head next to a sign: "The Bill Australia Can't Afford" along with "Higher taxes, more debt, a weak economy." The Liberals, finally, have conjured a smart, punchy line built around Bill's name. 'Unbelieva-Bill' was a short-lived Turnbull moniker, along with 'Electricity Bill'. It's a metaphor for their campaign in general. They seem better planned and more disciplined, have Bill firmly in their sights, and won't let up, at least not until the campaign kitty runs out, which, given Turnbull's departure and that of Julie Bishop, is a higher probability. At night, radio 3AW's Neil Mitchell is mocking Morrison in his television slot for his declaration that this is a choice between "me and Bill Shorten", but my overall impression is of how little the election is cutting through.

Granted, *The Australian* – Rupert Murdoch's request for a coronation-style one-on-one meeting having been knocked back by Shorten – is whipping itself into paroxysms of rage. "Real estate agents across the nation have declared war on Bill Shorten's negative gearing overhaul," *The Australian* screamed the day after the election was called.[88] Anyone would think Ben Chifley is back from the dead and intent upon nationalising housing. The Oz likes to back the winner, though, so what will their election-eve editorial do if the polls point towards a clear Labor victory? Nine News took 11 minutes to run the election, roughly the same as Channel Seven. In any case, it's mostly 'bubble' news: new MP citizenship woes and a feature on independents. Bill is in Bennelong. Why? It's an odd choice. What happened to the referendum on wages Labor promised only a few weeks ago? 'Everything is going up except for your wages.' It's an excellent line, but not being consistently deployed and not tied to a changing the government narrative. At a time when even the Reserve Bank governor is advocating for wage increases to lift consumption and economic growth, Labor's position isn't exactly radical. This isn't a change election, not yet I suspect.

My mood darkens over the weekend. I labour through a two-hour journey on public transport from Elsternwick to the Melbourne

Cricket Ground to see my footy team, the Brisbane Lions. We've started the season 3-zip, playing positive, attacking footy but today are mauled by a more experienced, ruthless team. Gulp. With the game effectively over at quarter time, I spend most of the match worrying over the election with my Lion-barracking mates, Bill's former Chief of Staff, Ken McPherson, and the Chair of the thinktank I head up, Dr Henry Pinskier. At half-time I send the following text to a number of Labor colleagues. "Our campaign worries me. This is not a change election. We have not offered a compelling material reason to change the government. Cancer treatment won't change a federal government. Coalition lines on risk are strong. We are not talking about the disunity on their side and, if so, it's half-hearted. We spoke of a referendum on wages yet three days in – nothing. It must be wages and the real economy and Labor managing it better for working people. It must be 'your lives have gotten worse because of that divided mob and you and your family will be better off with us'. I fear that unless Turnbull pipes up, and they start screwing up, we will get into trouble, quickly. Tell me I'm wrong. I desperately want to be wrong." No one demurred. Gulp. Then again, we are political weirdos; most of the crowd at the game hasn't tuned in to the election. An Essential survey conducted a full three weeks into the campaign reported that 16 per cent of respondents said they have not been paying any attention to the election campaign, with a further 29 per cent paying little attention. Only 19 per cent were fully tuned in to the contest, reporting they were paying a "lot of attention"; 36 per cent say they are paying "some" attention.[89]

On Sunday evening, the first election-time Newspoll comes out. The hypothetical "If an election were held today...?" is replaced with "how will you vote on May 18". Labor is steady at 52–48 after preferences, but the Coalition primary is up one to 39 per cent, Labor is unchanged on 39, the Greens 9, One Nation 4 and others 9. I suspect the 2PP is closer to 51-49 which is far tighter than Labor would want it in this contest.[90]

If governments lose elections it is as much a case of what they have done or haven't done, the inevitable scratches and dents collected along the voyage in office, as what the opposition says they threaten to do next if they were to be given another go. On the first campaign Monday the big story is an *Australian Financial Review* yarn on a report revealing that the Coalition will have to make cuts to health, education and other services of $40 billion a year by the end of the decade if it wants to balance the books and afford to implement its promised stage-two and stage-three income tax cuts.[91] The government is in a tricky position. Big end of town tax cuts aren't greatly popular: that much can be gleaned from how little they are spruiked. To be able to afford the radical flattening of the income tax scales that the Coalition is proposing in five years' time, which will put anyone earning up to $200,000 a year on a top marginal rate of 30 per cent, deep cuts will have to be made, or spending restraint exercised in a manner not seen for 50 years – certainly not during the life of this government.

The cancer policy is occupying space Labor could be using to talk about jobs and incomes – the 'referendum on wages'. I worry we might be trying to avoid talking about the economy; if we are, it won't work. A dark-humoured friend of mine seems to agree, texting to ask if the election is now a "referendum on cancer". Yet Labor is sticking with its focus on health spending. There is little doubt its policy to spend $2.3 billion helping pay for cancer treatments is popular. It's a visceral issue for sufferers, survivors and their relatives. The emotional trauma is exacerbated by fears over money. The 'Spanish Dancer' touches millions of Australians. I witnessed my Uncle die last year at its hands. My fiancé's Mum, a brilliant Jewish QC, was cut down in her early 50s. It's there in Bill's story – his Mum fought breast cancer – giving his messaging a sharper edge. On Day Five when he was thrown a curve-ball question from a cancer sufferer and former CFA volunteer, Shorten answered him in the press conference, and then spent some time with him afterwards, defusing the situation and probably winning a vote. He is good at this. Still the week-long cancer policy announcements are starting to irritate pundits, who argue it is being used to postpone debate on other issues, notably the economy and tax, as well as climate policy.

On the latter score, the Greens are pitching hard to their base, which they must, given their polling decline since its federal heyday of 2010 and disappointing state campaigns marred by division in New South Wales and Victoria. The Stop Adani convoy headed off from Hobart on Wednesday morning. The media is dominated by reports former leader Bob Brown likened coalminers to heroin dealers and Richard Di Natale will join the convoy over four days travelling from Melbourne to Brisbane, but will not go all the way to Clermont, a Queensland town once known for its links to the wool industry located near the mine site. Smart move. Smart or cynical, Di Natale later reprises the old Democrats' slogan of 'keeping the bastards honest' when making the Greens Party's pitch for the Senate in a speech at the National Press Club.[92] Brown once insisted his party aimed to 'replace the bastards', but the Greens have given up on the idea of being a party of government. Still, perhaps flying under the radar helps.

I have a feeling the Greens will poll well in inner-city seats, especially in Melbourne where the coal-carrying PM isn't popular and my local seat of Macnamara (formerly Melbourne Ports). Adani is a live issue. Labor's position is the equivalent of being half-pregnant. It won't get away with this in government, that's *if* it gets in.

***

Bill is having a torrid few days. A major leukemia announcement is overshadowed by stumbles on already announced changes to superannuation tax concessions for those earning more than $200,000 – typically framed as tax increases by the Coalition and its media mates – and over the economic impact of the party's climate change measures. It's allowed the Liberals to raise issues of trust and competence – he's 'shifty' and 'don't risk him' lines – and the old fear of mine about the baggage Shorten accrued from the leadership machinations of the Rudd-Gillard years re-surfaces. Shorten is right, it's impossible to quantify exactly, but that doesn't count in an election. It's the cover up rather than the crime which always kills you: some bright spark has decid-ed to delete the detail of Labor's changes to negative gearing and capital gains tax from the party's website, leading to further charges of shiftiness. On those pesky electric vehicles, Shorten has struggled with details of recharging times. The real worry is that the EV debate becomes a proxy for the campaign – La-bor policy is too expensive and impractical. This is the problem with 'progressive' politics in many respects. It starts from a per-spective that things can only get better, that there is a correct position, where people *should be* rather than *where they are*. As Maurice Glasman likes to say; "It's progressive" is the last thing you want to hear when you go to the doctor.

There is also a barney over Bill's barney with an aggressive re-porter from Channel 10. It began when the reporter complained that Shorten was only interested in talking about health. Bill's terse response confirms the truth behind the charge. As Mal-colm Farr observes in a column for *news.com.au*, Shorten's "campaign of the cancers" is so dominating Labor's election bid it is looking sick on other issues.[93] Of course, small stumbles can easily look like moments of high drama early in campaigns, especially when you are the frontrunner. It's best to get these stumbles out of the way early. Once nominations close we'll be hearing a lot more about Liberal gaffes and scandals – and also Labor ones. While Shorten's stumbles were unfortunate, Mor-rison and the Liberals made errors too. There are bloopers here and there – on Day 3 ScoMo says "ni hao" (hello in Chinese) to a Korean woman. Tony Abbott is at it again, not ruling out return-ing to lead the Liberals. George Christensen has been dubbed the MP for Manilla for using taxpayer-funded domestic flights to connect him to overseas flights. There is also a rambling, damaging interview by Barnaby Joyce on Radio National on the so-called Watergate affair. Of more concern, the Liberals have been caught out peddling departmental 'analyses' of Labor policies. When Peter Dutton made insensitive comments about his disabled Labor opponent in Dickson, Ali France, Morrison foolishly lets the story run for two-and-a-half days before Dutton apologises. Dutton, the ex-Queensland copper, might himself be placed in witness protection. Coalition gaffes and gadflies are however subsumed by the focus on Labor's slips. One Labor MP adds to the pile-on in anonymous comment for a Phillip Coorey *Australian Financial Review* piece: "we've got our arse hanging out in the breeze".[94]

This was never going to be repeat of 2016 even if Labor is presenting the same or similar policies. Last time around electors weren't seriously judging many policies as those likely to be enacted by a government – this time they are. Changes to negative gearing, capital gains tax, franking credits and trusts, as well as not passing on tax cuts to the wealthiest Australians and big business, each involve annoying various constituencies. Negative gearing reform, for example, was a winning argument back in 2016 when the housing market was booming in every eastern seaboard capital. Now with the bubble bursting and prices falling it's perceived very differently.

Labor's calculation is that those who will benefit from the extra revenue outnumber those who do not. But I sense this creates a juicy target – a succulent meal? – for a rival skilled at mounting fear campaigns, particularly as the Coalition appears to have got its act together. Morrison is an effective campaigner, even if the daggy dad act stretches credulity. He is everywhere acting as everyman: shooting pool in Corangamite, playing lawn bowls, inspecting a carrot farm, sipping beer with punters – one crowd taunt him for not skulling a frothy Hawke-style – cheering on Winx one day; Cronulla the next. Turnbull is quietly ensconced in New York, save for a Twitter foray urging the government to set up a fund to help rebuild the Notre Dame Cathedral; it's left to merchant banker son Alex to fly the family flag on the same medium. The absence of Turnbull is good for Coalition unity; bad for Labor's assertion they govern for the 'top end of town'. It worked well when multimillionaire Turnbull was prime minister but doesn't resonate so much in Morrison's case. At the very least, his feisty campaign has precluded the possibility of a landslide Coalition defeat.

The Coalition won the first full week of the campaign. Labor has talked endlessly about health, teasing out its flagship cancer policy announcement. This isn't enough to change a government. It's overly cautious, certainly in its lack of focus on the government's weakest point: intra-party division and living standards. Nonetheless there is a long way to go and much of the debate hasn't touched the change factors at play. This is an election about fairness – the headline stats haven't changed and Labor is proposing big fixes. This is a generational election and Labor's policy pitch to younger voters is strong. This is an election about leadership: I suspect the public are done with Messiahs and in a mood to punish the Libs' five and a half years of leadership indulgences. Troy Bramston from The Oz, with whom I've had my disagreements, makes the essential point: the Coalition could plausibly 'win' every single week of the campaign, but lose the election in convincing fashion.[95]

Week 2 – A referendum on wages (finally)

Morrison is staying negative. Yes, he is arguing that the Liberals are superior economic managers, his focus is on broad economic management, on the return to surplus, debt repayment, and aggregate employment growth, and he prefaces adverts and public appearances with the statement 'We live in the best country in the world.' But ... there's always a but. Labor is a risk. It's policies amount to a "tax grab", it will trash the budget and the economy. Granted, Morrison isn't attacking more spending on cancer treatments, or better educational opportunities, and addressing climate change. The PM is savvy enough not to attack those goals directly. Instead, he is attacking Labor's tax initiatives to pay for them and pointing to Labor's record in government.

Labor's campaign is too positive for my liking. It hasn't talked about the past five years of dysfunction, broken promises and a stagnating economy under the Liberals. There isn't a recurring line that returning the Liberals will not be a cost-free exercise. People – Malcolm Turnbull at least – might complain about last election's Mediscare campaign, but it worked. In the *Herald Sun* former state Labor minister Theo Theophanous argues that it needs to be adapted to counter the Coalition's claim to superior economic management: not a single budget surplus despite once warning of a debt and deficit disaster, gross debt doubled, 1.8 million Australians are under-employed, wages growth is at record lows, and power bills are up 30 per cent, despite the Coalition's 2014 axing of the carbon tax and donut of an energy policy.[96]

Wages are the most confounding omission so far. The 'referendum on wages' is fought for a day here and there, but not consistently. During the campaign's second weekend, Shorten vows to make penalty rates a priority of industrial relations reform, with changes to be enacted in the first 100 days of a Labor government. In the days that follow he promises 2.6 million casual workers an easier pathway to permanent employment, as part of a widening overhaul of the industrial relations system, and to make it more expensive to hire skilled foreign workers, and an expansion of apprenticeships to address skills shortages and legislating domestic violence leave. Then a jarring element of Bill's personality emerges: call it his instinct for consensus, or his need to be liked, or rather not to displease. Confronted by a coal export terminal engineer in Gladstone – probably a manager and not a wage earner – Shorten says Labor would look at tax breaks for Australians earning more than $200,000 a year. Why not just tell him that providing such tax breaks isn't Labor's focus now? Labor is on the side of the 90 per cent of workers earning less than $100,000. It is left to Opposition workplace relations spokesman Brendan O'Connor to say Bill was "being courteous" and "polite".[97] I'm struck by the lack of cut-through advertisements by the ACTU. Its secretary, Sally McManus, has injected badly needed energy and strategic focus into the peak-union body since coming to the job in 2017. There are rallies a plenty, but the 'Change the Rules' campaign lacks the hard-edged, family-values tone which hallmarked 'Your Rights at Work'. I suspect it is because CtR seems to speak to union rights and rules rather than working people's immediate economic needs. But the best own goal all week is kicked by employers. In The Oz, a small business lobby tsar admits that cuts to Sunday penalty rates had not created one new job or prompted business to give extra hours to workers – so why then were they cut at all?

Perhaps more confounding is Labor's silence on a rise in the unemployment figures before Easter. 17,000 Australians lost their jobs in March and, in an election in which the public mood is anxious about the economy, not a word from the Opposition? "Unemployment is up and wages are down – change the government" texts a friend, and it's as good a refrain as any we are using so far. I knew this data was set for release during the campaign, did CHQ? The 'grid' has a lot to answer for.

But who is tuning in, in this the second week? It begins with the Easter break, restarts briefly, and is interrupted again by Anzac Day and is dominated by the horrific terrorist bombings in Sri Lanka. I had in 2014, eaten in the very room at one of the very hotel's where the terrorists stride. Me? My third child is born during the lull. We are on the precipice of changing the government after five and a half years – I'm changing nappies after a similar hiatus. And yet I can't break the habit. Out of frustration I send Bill a message one evening – part-critique, part-pep talk: "Don't forget what you do best – it always works. Hit their weakest points – everything going up except for people's wages & the disunity of six years. Can they be trusted not to change leaders again - will it be Abbott or Dutton again? And don't let up. Use it to build the narrative for changing government. You can bring this home."

The Easter break and Anzac Day are over. By the reckoning of the respective campaign teams, voters will be paying more attention and forming their judgement – including ever greater numbers of Australians voting early, which began on April 29. Bigger policy announcements will follow, Morrison and Shorten will face off in two leadership debates, and we can be sure of more scandals, given the fact that nominations have closed – i.e. a candidate can't be taken off the ballot paper. Or maybe the big policy announcements won't flow. There is another election being fought – seat-by-seat battles on local issues. Many of the government's candidates are running on what they have done for local roads, sports facilities or car parks, or styling themselves as 'Modern Liberal', and scaling back their use of party logos. It's easily the most meaningful three-word slogan the Libs have dreamt up: Not Tony Abbott.

Week Three: Thai holiday snaps

The campaign proper has begun. Shorten senses voters are tuning in and promises to spend $34 billion over 10 years on childcare worker wages, family childcare subsidies and, in possibly the biggest extension of Medicare in generations, free dental care for pensioners. It's not so much a reset than a mega reminder to voters that they should see that this election as not a personality contest but a policy match. In this Shorten is playing on the same ground he has occupied for five years. He opposed cuts in the Coalition's May 2014 budget in favour of higher spending on health, education, pensions and family tax benefits, but Morrison has backtracked, in part, on these Abbott-era measures. Tax is more problematic. Labor has the edge with voters who earn less than $48000, the Coalition appeals to those on more than $90000: that's if they are prepared to wait until 2022 for their cut, and aren't also interested in money being spent on services such as childcare, which is especially the case for those with partners earning considerably less money. But has Labor left it too late to spell out to voters why it is generating extra revenue to pay for its spending promises? Morrison cannot match Labor's spending measures given his commitment to company and personal tax cuts. It's an odd predicament for Morrison – massively outspent but unable to show Australians how the Coalition will deliver a better bottom line in the budget over the next electoral cycle. Though maybe *not* spending billions is *the strategy*. Shorten's tactical nous, according to some in the media, has re-emerged: the big spending measures made on the weekend will provide the Labor leader with a bevy of talking points for tomorrow's first televised debate with Scott Morrison.

There is a nostalgic element to the Coalition's campaign with the appearance of John Howard the day before the first debate at a campaign rally in the key seat of Reid. I wonder if Morrison is too deferential to the old man, too frightened to craft his own agenda. It is no coincidence that on Sunday, Morrison simultaneously announces a cap on Australia's refugee intake. But the heat seems to have gone out of the refugee debate, which is somewhat surprising given the brouhaha over medical transfers which dominated the last month of the 2018 parliament and the first months of the political year and saw the government spend millions reopening the Christmas Island detention centre, before its quick closure. Privately, I was gobsmacked Labor made an issue out of Medevac – legislation which aimed to bring refugees on Manus and Nauru to Australia for medical care – at least in terms of using it as the issue to embarrass the minority Morrison government. I wonder if it hasn't stuck in voter's minds.

The debate comes and goes, though it scarcely warrants the

label. There are, absurdly, three hosts, including Perth football identity Basil Zempilas. The two leaders, shown in split screen, stare awkwardly at the camera. Morrison is in attack mode – he has no other option given the paucity of a campaign agenda, other than to say he isn't Shorten. Bill starts awkwardly but, as is his habit with these things, warms up as he goes – I've seen it firsthand at town hall events where he has to be literally dragged out by minders – particularly when questions are directed from the audience of swinging voters. But for the most part the lines are well-worn: it's the Coalition's 'don't change, don't risk Labor' versus Labor's 'the cost of not changing, not acting on wages and climate, is too great'. Ducking and weaving when ScoMo actually wants to make the debate a debate, Bill hammers their key weaknesses towards the end: "The reality is that in the last six years when you voted for Tony Abbott you ended up getting Malcolm Turnbull, when you voted for Malcolm Turnbull last time you got Mr Morrison. When you vote for Mr Morrison this time, who knows, you might get Clive Palmer or Pauline Hanson. The chaos has to stop. But as important as the instability of the current government is the question: is this a strong economy for who? Who benefits at the moment?" There is a bit of mongrel too, and a riposte to the ScoMo everyday man act when the PM hones in on a potential 'gotcha' moment on the price of electric vehicles. "I can tell you how electric cars cost more – it's 28,000 bucks for the same type of car," Morrison charges, to which Shorten shot back: "That's great. We've got a PM spending his time in the motor pages – that's super." Morrison responded in turn: "That's where most Australians often spend their time, mate." Shorten replied: "I am not talking about who won the fifth at Flemington, digger."[98] The Perth studio audience judge Shorten the winner. Crucially he doesn't make any clangers, half the trick with these forums, and most pundits declare the debate a Shorten win or a draw, whatever that means, given that it won't change most votes. Afterwards there is some confected rubbish over 'perve-gate' – Finance Minister Mathias Cormann is falsely accused on social media of "perving" at Chloe Shorten. The only outrage industry seemingly missing is an animal liberation army of protestors fuming about the killing off of Nine's infamous leaders' debate 'worm'.

****

That sound is the heart palpitations racing in Labor's CHQ. Newspoll has tightened. Labor would still win an election based on the 51:49 result, but the numbers will make its operatives nervous. Counter-intuitively, the Coalition's primary vote has slipped back to just 38 per cent.[99] Can ScoMo win with a two-party vote that low? Sooner or later Morrison's charmed run, free of hard questions, will end surely? The small-target strategy is going to lead to questions about what he plans to do if returned and who will appear in cabinet. Questions about his missing-in-action Environment Minister, Melissa Price, are becoming more insistent, especially as the government, off the back of some dodgy numbers peddled by a Liberal Party propagandist, is running a new climate change cost scare campaign. I'm beginning to suspect Morrison has overcompensated for Turnbull's overly 'positive' 2016 campaign. His campaign could do with a semblance of positivity, perhaps even a new policy here or there.

'United Australia Party's official campaign launch event. Watch it here!' I decline the opportunity afforded by a SMS text from Clive Palmer's $60m campaign extravaganza. It's good for a laugh, though, as I glimpse a message nestled underneath, also sent from the 'UAP', sent back on January 18: 'When elected, United Australia Party will ban unsolicited political text messages which Labor & Liberal have allowed.'

It's impossible to ignore Palmer, self-proclaimed mega-rich and megalomaniac anti-politician. His saturation television adverts proclaim past policy outcomes he had no involvement in, engage in racist dog-whistling about the Chinese, style him as a feminist champion of working women, promise fantastic outcomes such as fast rail and nuclear power, all of which will be realised when his party takes office, or so Clive says. It's Orwellian but he has done it before. He effectively bought the balance of power in the Senate in 2013, spending $28.9m on the election and the Western Australian Senate rerun, most of which went on saturation advertising. Back then, Palmer won his lower house seat and three spots in the Senate. Under a preference deal between Palmer and the Coalition, the former would direct preferences to the Coalition in House seats in return for Coalition Senate preferences. The deal stinks and while there is a chance UAP preference recommendations will lift the Coalition's national two-party vote, there is a risk to the Coalition of doing a deal with someone as disliked by the general public as Palmer, at least in the Southern states.

The prospect of Palmer entering the senate is astonishing given his record, notably the collapse of Queensland Nickel. Eight hundred jobs in Townsville were lost when the company went bust in early 2016. Palmer thumbed his nose at the sacked workers and their families. He refused to pay the $70 million of entitlements legally owed to them: "I have no personal responsibility, I retired from business over three years ago", he stated, despite profits being redirected from the company to other Palmer businesses.[100] Instead taxpayers footed the bill including the people who found themselves out of a job. Some workers have never recovered. Despite this, Palmer is expected to spend $50 million by campaign's end as he openly boasts that he is worth "four-thousand-million dollars". He is wrong as usual – it's a cool $1.8 billion or 1.8 thousand million dollars. But who's counting? It will be an indictment on our democracy if he is elected. God help ScoMo if he needs to work with Palmer should he win. Accepting UAP references is riskier than signing an employment contract with Clive. It's not only the Coalition giving Clive an easy run – The Australian's reportage is soft, while Newspoll has included the UAP in its list of minor parties, no doubt lifting its projected primary and guaranteeing more media coverage.[101]

The election is bogged down in scandal quite aside from Clive. Scott Morrison is egged by some goose at a Country Women's Association event in Albury. A Liberal candidate in Tasmania has quit the campaign because of anti-Muslim and anti-refugee comments. Another candidate in Victoria was dumped for making anti-Islam comments online and yet another quit for posting anti-gay rants. Labor's Melbourne candidate has quit over lewd jokes he posted on his Facebook page. Earlier in the week, Labor dumped one of its NT senate candidates, Wayne Kurnoth, for posting bizarre anti-Semitic conspiracy theories. PHON senate candidate Steve Dickson is out, too, after footage of him drunkenly cavorting in a Washington DC strip club was screened on Channel Nine's *A Current Affair*. Another PHON candidate Ross MacDonald also quit after the revelations of his Facebook page devoted to sleazy Thailand holiday pics – cue to a teary Pauline Hanson television interview in which she expertly plays the victim, again. Pundits like to point to the immortality of social media. Me, I'm eternally confounded by the Coalition's attitude to Muslims. No doubt some irredentist elements of the Coalition and their media cheerleaders think anti-Islam dog-whistling is smart politics. While we should be careful not to stereotype a diverse ethno-religious grouping, many of the 500,000 plus Australian Muslim community are social conservatives – consult the seat-by-seat results of the 2017 marriage equality survey. Why would they vote for a party that scapegoats them? The Libs have form: it was a similar form of Protestant sectarianism which made Roman Catholics baulk at voting for the various incarnations of anti-Labor over the twentieth century. Yet, when the sectarianism stopped, they voted and joined the Coalition – one even ended up becoming PM in the case of Tony Abbott. Why can't they get this into their heads with respect to the heterogenous Muslim community?

Amid the buffoonery the week is best called a draw. Labor has drawn some heat – and perhaps bled some votes – over its detailed policy manifesto. The Coalition's unrelentingly negative campaign has worked so far, but the danger is voters will switch off. 'Where the bloody hell is Scott Morrison's agenda?', they might ask. Or, ominously, the 2019 election has become a referendum on Labor and Bill.

Week Four: Space Invaders

It's Scott Morrison's Mark Latham moment, they say. The Sky News 'People's Debate' is held in Brisbane midweek. The sparsely watched event is dominated by debate over Labor's policy agenda and, as it happened, Morrison's debating technique. Morrison was his usual assertive self, perhaps a little too much. In response to Morrison's gesticulations and physically proximity, a grinning Shorten declared to laughter that the PM was "a classic space invader". It's not really a "Latham moment" – a reference to the ex-Labor leader-cum-One Nation NSW MLC famously fierce shaking of John Howard's hand in the 2004 campaign. Shorten's pitch was familiar, too. "The economy is not working in the interests of working and middle class people."[102] Again his countless town hall meetings stood him in good stead. When the subject of youth mental health was raised, Shorten asked the audience to put up their hands if they'd known a family affected by suicide. Morrison was among the many who did so. It's another 'win' to Bill. Then again, he can win all three debates and lose the election.

Labor's campaign launch is held at Brisbane's Convention Centre two days later on May 5. The launch features the Go-Betweens song, "Spring Rain" with its lyrics "When will change come?" Except, with 13 days to go; it still doesn't feel like a change election but a gruelling seat by seat contest. It's tighter than it should be. The launch itself is low-key, and certainly not a coronation event, à la Kevin Rudd in 2007. In tune with Labor's campaign, the team, stability and unity are the dominant notes played here. The shadow cabinet was seated earnestly on stage behind the speakers. Save for a sick Bob Hawke, the Labor ex-prime ministers club Paul Keating, Kevin Rudd and Julia Gillard are all there –

the latter duo doing an admirable job of bearing each other's company – ramming home the launch's unity theme. (Though the uncomfortable presence, together, of Rudd and Gillard also reminded viewers of the fraught, recent history of Labor in power.) Women are centre stage – proceedings were kicked off by Queensland Labor premier Annastacia Palaszczuk, Senate leader Penny Wong, Deputy Tanya Plibersek, and finally Chloe Shorten. It's modern in another sense. Indigenous dancers were part of the Welcome to Country. Pat Dodson – who would be Indigenous affairs minister in a Shorten government – pledged Labor would "walk with First Nations peoples". It's hard to imagine such scenes playing out in the equivalent Liberal campaign launch. Then again what some might argue to be a case of progressive virtue-signalling won't sway the votes of punters ultimately casting their ballot papers on the basis of the economy. They don't have Hawkie either, even if the old fella is absent. "Bob, we love you", Shorten declared to cheers, "and in the next 13 days we're going to do this for you".[103] It's a good speech: casting Labor as the party for working people and the government as mates of the privileged. Only Labor can change the status quo, so change the government. Shorten speaks well but the obsessive focus on health continues. Labor would direct $500 million to emergency department waiting times. There's an announcement of a tax break for business to hire both younger and older workers, which draws sustained applause when Shorten speaks of the injustice and angst felt by older unemployed workers. It's a theme, through the unscheduled media attention to his late mother, we'll hear much about in coming days.

The next day is maddeningly dominated by Newspoll and Paul Keating. Newspoll has the ALP leading the Coalition by an unchanged 51-49 per cent on a two-party basis which is something of a relief; the bleeding has been stemmed.[104] Nine Media's Ipsos says the same thing, although it continues to grossly overstate the Greens' primary. Had it been 50-50 all hell would have broken loose. Speaking of hell breaking loose, in characteristic style,

Keating told an interviewer with the ABC the Prime Minister was "a fossil with a baseball cap".[105] Raw meat for the true believers, but then Keating provided the government with a chance to shift the debate on to national security, declaring Australia's security chiefs to be "nutters" who should be sacked because they were damaging relations with China. Fortunately Shorten manages to shut the debate down. It's a reminder of Keating's polarising nature: he's great for internal Labor consumption but a harder mouthful to swallow for many swinging voters.

On 7 May Morrison dodges his own bullet when the Reserve Bank decides to keep interest rates on hold, with Shorten suggesting the prospect of a rate cut showed that the economy was "wallowing in mediocrity".[106] The release of ABS data covering wages and jobs growth just two days before the election proper will be more than interesting. The same day the one millionth Australian cast their vote in the election, eleven days before the actual ballot. Early voting records are being smashed. Higher pre-poll voting, according to some cynical pundits, suggests that voters no longer listen to what politicians say this close to an election. They were mistaken.

The Labor leader performed strongly on the ABC's *Q&A* program on the Monday of the second last week, fielding questions on a range of issues from the audience. Notably, he recounted his mother Ann's experience to explain his approach to political life, saying he was driven to ensure that all Australians were given equality of opportunity. Two days later the *Daily Telegraph*'s front page screamed 'Mother of Invention', its lead article alleging Shorten had omitted details about his mother's legal career. He was allegedly "loose on detail".[107] In one of the most compelling moments of the election campaign thus far, at a hospital event doorstop, a tearful Shorten derided the Tele's story as "gotcha shit" and spoke at length about his mother's experience of going to university in her 40s to realise a thwarted dream to become a barrister.[108] The story was factually incorrect:

Bill has often spoken of his 'brilliant and clever' mother as a key influence in his life, pointing out that while she went to university, instead of pursuing law, as she wanted, Ann needed to take the teacher scholarship to look after the rest of the kids. The news story backfired, generating sympathy for Shorten, even from the Prime Minister, though the yarn was surely placed by the Liberals. Tellingly, the *Telegraph*'s sister paper, Melbourne's *Herald Sun*, did not run the story at all. Its columnist Andrew Bolt, no friend of Labor, pulled no punches. "There is no invention here. That she decades later realised her dream does not negate that sacrifice."[109] Bill's presser dominated the evening news bulletins, possibly engaging disengaged voters. The article and Bill's response prompted anger on social media, with Twitter users sharing their mothers' stories under the #MyMum hashtag. I write my own opinion piece for *The Monthly* in response – once a Shorten staffer always a Shorten staffer, you might say.[110]

It won't win the election but there was the real Bill, to purloin a phrase, fired-up, passionate, a touch vulnerable, wounded, himself. Finally. The emotional rebuttal humanised him and allowed him to talk more about two issues that resonate with many Australians – the struggle and sacrifice of working mothers, and the problem of age discrimination – and personalise the overarching Labor campaign theme of fairness. "I choose to give you that last bit of the battle of her time at the bar because my mum would want me to say to older women in Australia – that just because you've got grey hair, just because you didn't go to a special private school, just because you don't go to the right clubs, just because you're not part of some back-slapping boys' club, doesn't mean you should give up". "She's brilliant", said Shorten, his voice cracking. "And that's what drives me."[111] During the Royal Commission into Trade Unions and Registered Organisations (TURC)'s hearings Bill Kelty warned Shorten: "you have to absorb pain" to become PM.[112] But would pain be enough?

Labor 'won' the week in pundit land and Bill the third debate.

The Coalition are running out of puff. I convince myself I've seen how this movie ends. In 2013, Rudd's campaign literally ran out of things to talk about, producing thought-bubbles such as a tax-free zone in the Northern Territory. Stepping off a plane in Tasmania, the first Team Shorten heard of it was a news alert which flashed simultaneously across our phones. I knew at that moment all hope was gone – Morgan that day had us behind 53-47, a figure more or less repeated in Newspoll and elsewhere. Others aren't convinced. I still remember Bob Ellis's call a few minutes later. 'Nick, tell Bill it's bullshit. The real polls are 53-47 our way. Newspoll and Morgan won't get away with trying to steal the election'. 'Sure, comrade', I lie to Bob, 'I'll pass your message to Bill'.

Week Five: 'The Promise of Australia'

Friday, May 10: Labor has released its full costings. Irresponsible tax loopholes used by the wealthy and big corporations are closed, tax cuts to high-income earners not pursued, generating substantial additional tax revenue to spent funding health and childcare and directed toward higher surpluses than those projected by the Coalition. Unlike 2016, when Labor proposed to have a deficit of about $16.5 billion more across the forward estimates than that in the official Pre-election Economic and Fiscal Outlook (PEFO), Chris Bowen and Jim Chalmers, Labor's key economic team, are bettering the Coalition's bottom line. Labor hopes its budget numbers will help counter the government's line on economic responsibility, though the potential for last minute scare campaigns around the so-called 'Retiree Tax' et al remains. The Oz's ideological guru Paul Kelly proclaims that Labor's numbers show Bill Shorten is "ready to govern".[113] He has sniffed the wind, but his colleagues haven't got the memo: the paper's associate editor and former Liberal staffer Chris Kenny and others are doubling down on the Ann Shorten story – it's evidence, they assert, of a leftist campaign to silence debate – they were only ever trying to tell an Australian success story!

It's symptomatic really of how out of touch and irrational what purports to be conservative thought in this country has become. Most evidence is suggesting that the Australian economy is not as strong as Morrison and his cheerleaders are wont to claim. The Reserve Bank is forecasting year-on-year economic growth in the 2018-19 financial year of just 1.7 per cent, the lowest since the depths of the global financial crisis. Household income growth is slowing. Wages, as the release of the March figures show, have been stagnant for nine months. The construction sector is falling in a heap. The best Morrison can offer up is that he has delivered: a budget surplus *next year*.

You wouldn't know any of this from the Liberals' Mother's Day launch in Melbourne – you couldn't make this up after the Ann Shorten fracas. It's really the Morrison launch though, focussed on the PM and his family. Outside, protesters dressed as giant inflatable poop emojis cause a hullaballoo. Minimalistic, low-key, sparsely attended, the launch generates two tangible moments: the first, Morrison's line that his "vision for this country as your Prime Minister is to keep the Promise of Australia to all Australians", which sounds a bit Hillsong-ish before the speechwriter in me realises that it was ripped from an 1980s Bob Hawke speech. The second – aside from a well-publicised promise to spend $4bn on constructing EastLink in Melbourne – is a policy shocker, another first home buyer's subsidy scheme targeting younger voters, perhaps for the first time this campaign. Morrison promises that the government will underwrite the mortgages of a select number of Australians who aren't able to put together a standard twenty per cent deposit. Labor matches the policy within hours, neutralising the issue, but I wonder whether it hasn't booby-trapped itself in the process. Does the Liberal Party even stand for anything anymore? The IPA and most economists think it is a terrible idea. Yet bastions of free market thought take up the cudgel of state socialism: 'ScoMo's home run' x 2, 'Home run: PM's property bet', 'Home Stretch' are the *Daily Tele*, *Herald Sun*, *The Australian* and *Hobart Mercury* front covers the next day. In the same coverage, the latest Newspoll has Labor maintaining a 51-49 per cent 2PP lead. Shorten closes on Morrison as preferred PM. Both sides increased their primary votes by one point: the Coalition on 39; Labor 37.[114] My bleeding heart calls it for Labor and I foolishly pronounce as much to friends.

The leaders and their entourages zig-zag the country this final week. Bill holds a rally in Western Sydney at the site of Whitlam's 1972 'It's Time' campaign event. It's one big ode to Gough, rallying the faithful, and full of talk of change. Bill speaks well, but I don't like it – he should be channelling Hawke, the consensus leader, in my view, rather than Gough, who is still seen as divisive in many parts of Australia. The television and radio advert blackout kicks-in on Wednesday evening, though the Facebook bombardment continues. Sure, there are moments of drama like when Labor's Belinda Hassan, who is taking on George Christensen in Dawson, is suspected of being the target of an arson attack. Keating and Howard pop up once more, like ageing rock stars on never-ending comeback tours. Barnaby Joyce is tweeting as though he's twelve pints down at the local pub, while the party he once led is ding donging with the Liberals. There is a fracas over whether the PM thinks gays will go to 'hell' or not, mostly played out in the pages of *The Australian* where the likes of Chris Kenny are making out as if it is some sort of secular-inspired inquisition. The newspaper's frontpage makes the remarkable claim: 'Shorten ignites Holy War'. That said, I wish Labor wasn't making an issue of the Prime Minister's religion this final week. Clive Palmer might miss election day altogether: he's been spotted holidaying in Fiji. I wonder if he'll talk to the locals about their government's negotiation of a free trade agreement with the Chinese or signing up to their vast Belt and Road Initiative. Maybe he'll be joined by Channel Ten personality Kerri-Anne Kennerley who tells morning viewers "If Bill Shorten gets in, it's the end of life as we know it."[115]

'Bob Hawke has died'

Two days out from the election I'm relaxing with baby on the couch watching tele. 'Bob Hawke has died', the newsreader announces matter of factly. The hairs on my neck and arms stand to attention in the manner of a military parade. A single tear ambles down my right cheekbone, before picking up speed and dropping upon my neck. As a child I grew up with Hawke as Prime Minister. I didn't quite know what he and his mate Paul were banging on about on the TV, but I instinctively knew it was important. Bob – or the 'Silver Bodgie' as Mum and Dad called him to my bemusement – was instinctively Australian. He changed this country forever and for the better. He did more than that – he preserved Australia as a fair and decent country to live. I don't know what this means for the election – it's certainly not going to win or lose it for Labor – but it adds to the strange pre-election vibe. Labor campaigning comes to a halt on Friday, and tributes pour in, Shorten pays his respects to Hawke's wife Blanche D'Alpuget; the Labor faithful gather for drinks at the Curtin Hotel in Melbourne.

I don't sleep much the night before the election and it's not just my newborn baby. I feel uneasy despite a number of election-eve polls indicating a sound Labor victory. In between parenting duties, I hand out at the local primary school in Caulfield South, which captures voters in two seats: Macnamara, a three-cornered tussle between Labor, Liberal and the Greens and blue-ribbon Liberal Goldstein. It's dead. It's not just the lack of voters – and many of the suburb's Jewish voters will have pre-polled given that the election is, as usual, held on the Sabbath – but there doesn't seem to be any real enthusiasm or hostility towards any of the party volunteers. I'm struck again, however, by the Liberals' negative posters: 'The Bill Australia Can't Afford'. Maybe it's just pre-election jitters but I can't help thinking this isn't the advertising of a losing side. I finish up at 4pm – in less than four hours the result will be known.

The numbers start rolling in. Tasmania is bad. It appears two seats in the Apple Isle are gone by 7pm. Queensland is diabolical. Victoria is a Curate's Egg and there are no tangible gains being made in NSW. 'Calm down!' a friend texts when I hint at the unthinkable: Labor isn't going to get there. By 8pm it looks as if Labor will need to rely on Western Australia. 9pm: it's over. Labor can't win. Bill won't become PM. This campaign witnessed the Liberals do what they have singularly failed hitherto: they didn't underestimate Shorten and they outcampaigned him. In the wee hours I re-read Bill's take on the 2004 election which showed Labor ahead in the polls heading into the campaign. "Labor released a lot of policies with no punch ... while the Coalition relentlessly hammered home a few key messages. The Liberals out-spent and out-targeted Labor with their TV ads ... I have not yet spoken to a member of the Australian Workers Union who can explain Labor's tax and family policy. Regrettably, negative campaigning by the Coalition worked." I feel sick, literally. In the election's aftermath, Blue Labour thinker and scholar Adrian Pabst, neatly summarises my thoughts: "The tragedy of [Shorten's] leadership was that he ended up embracing the very progressive politics that alienates sections of the working and middle-class voters who are more socially conservative and want a radically reforming Labor government, which offers working Australians a share of prosperity and the good life."[116]

Shorten takes to the stage in Melbourne at around 10pm to concede defeat. Amid a sea of blue, and a good sprinkling of the blue rinse set, Scott Morrison claims victory at what was meant to be a Sydney-based wake soon afterwards. Decked out in the party's traditional red, Labor's true believers are feeling decidedly blue. The Prime Minister's speech is eventually muted. Laborites should feel blue, but not for the reasons they think. Getting a serious case of the blues is the answer to Labor's 2019 disaster.

5

ONCE WERE LABORISTS

'Something old, something new, something borrowed, something blue'. At first glance this old English rhyme sits oddly amid a discussion of the crisis of Australian Labor. Yet it is a more than handy guide to the task confronting social democrats locally and internationally. The Cold War's end and the GFC haunts Laborists and the union movement the world over. The latter failed to realise predictions of a social democratic renaissance. 2019 shows that Labor is not immune from the fate of its social democratic comrades. Australia has for the time being avoided the Trump/Brexit style phenomenon of disaffected working- and middle-class Australians turning *en masse* to populist parties of the Right. But they are swinging in that direction. Preference flows from far-Right populist parties to the Coalition in 2019 were critical. Nonetheless Australia's would-be emulators of Donald Trump and UKIP, formerly lead by Nigel Farage, who now heads up the Brexit Party, are poorly suited to the task of replicating Trump's success. Whether it is Pauline Hanson, Mark Latham and Cory Bernardi, they are obsessed with pursuing tangential 'culture wars' rather than hip-pocket concerns of working people. The populist Right has failed to fatally split the social democratic base (though compulsory, preferential voting surely plays a role as does the major party consensus on immigration and multiculturalism), in part because Australian Labor remains a more materialist and less cosmopolitan entity than most Western social democratic parties, owing to the greater institutional role of unions, no matter their well-documented decline in density. They continue to anchor the party's policy focus. To remain as such Labor's primary campaign focus must remain fixed on wages, jobs and economic management, as a means of appealing to the nation as a whole.

Neither the GFC nor the experience of the Rudd-Gillard governments nor the Shorten-era can be singled out for our local Laborite malaise. The past three decades of polling are clear and depressing for Labor. After 1993 Labor is on a clear downwards trajectory. By contrast the trend for the Coalition is stable, with no overall decline above one per cent. The trend for minor parties is up, almost exclusively at the expense of Labor. Between 1993 to 2010 it has haemorrhaged votes – though not lower house seats – to the Greens as the 'progressive' middle class switched their votes on the basis of post-material issues such as climate change and the treatment of refugees. More damaging has been the trend operating between 2013 to 2019 as a portion of Labor's lower income, non-tertiary educated, blue-collar constituency moved to minor parties like UAP, One Nation and other minor parties. Speaking directly to the cases of Queensland and Western Australia in 2019, academic Paul Rodan comments: "a decision by workers on [lower] levels of income to vote for the conservatives (even if via preferences) could well be consistent with a rational assessment of their economic self-interest. Labor's sketchily detailed promise of higher wages seems to have failed to trump voters' concern with immediate job security, as symbolised by the Adani project. And, given that the labour movement itself was conflicted over Adani, the mining union was less equipped to perform its usual role of maximising solidarity at election time. Having voted non-Labor for the first time, a proportion of blue-collar voters may now be comfortable with that choice, and may not easily be lured back to Labor."[117] If the current trend continues, federal Labor's primary will drop below 30 per cent by 2025 and possibly earlier. As the Victorian ALP assistant state secretary Kos Samaras puts it: "This is a multi-generational problem for Labor. The blame is multi-generational."[118] The solutions, too, are multi-generational, sourced from ideas and policies generated abroad but also found within

Labor's native traditions.

The very survival of social democracy demands transnational collaboration between parties, a hallmark of social democracy at its best in the past, and a guiding theme to its future.[119] There is a long tradition among Western left-of-centre parties looking to the electoral strategies and thinking of fellow-travellers. Australian Labor's precocious electoral growth during the 1890s and 1900s won the attention of European observers and, in turn, owed much to Fabian and other socialist thought emanating from Britain as well as its adaptation of the strategies and language of British Chartism, American-style populism and continental socialist theory. The Curtin and Chifley government's post-World War Two reconstruction program and extension of the welfare state looked to developments in the Anglosphere – notably the UK's 1942 Beveridge Report and Roosevelt's 1930s New Deal. It married Labor's older belief in modifying market outcomes in pursuit of social justice with the British economist John Maynard Keynes' call for increased government activity to smooth out the economic cycle amid the widespread fear that the boom resulting from the war would be followed by scarcity, unemployment and perhaps another Depression. A few decades later Gough Whitlam drew, even if unconsciously so, upon British Labour intellectual Anthony Crosland's revisionism of the 1950s, as he modernised the ALP in the late 1960s. He confronted the party's flat-earthers, notably forces associated with the Victorian left-winger Bill Hartley, who ignored or denied the seismic changes to Australian society after World War Two. The party's organisational structure was reformed, and its membership widened to include middle-class 'progressives'. Following Crosland's cue, Labor policy was overhauled, focussing on expanding opportunity rather than the traditional focus on income redistribution and a naïve belief in the virtues of state ownership. Conversely, British New Labour's Third Way thinking, as championed by Tony Blair, with echoes in the policies of Gerhard Schroeder and others in the 1990s, was influenced by the experience of the Hawke/Keating Labor governments the previous decade. Indeed, Blair as Shadow Home Secretary and Gordon Brown, as Shadow Chancellor, had visited Australia in Opposition to learn directly about the Hawke Labor governance model. In turn, Third Wayism was picked up by Labor thinkers and then up-and-coming MPs such as Mark Latham. Scandinavia, too, provided policy inspiration for some thinkers, as has Germany's social market economy.

A further example illustrates that social democratic ideas have never existed in a national vacuum. In 1899, the German revisionist theorist Eduard Bernstein famously suggested that social democratic politics, rather than having some ultimate end-goal, was more about the collective struggle in itself. As he insisted "the movement is everything". To be sure, Bernstein's own views evolved from contact with the socialism of Marx and Engels and, critically, his engagement – intellectual and fraternal – with English Fabians and ethical socialism. At the same time, we must be aware of the social democracy's national nuances and cognisant of how ideas are reapplied to particular settings. To paraphrase a famous definition of the concept of social class, social democracy arose in the same way in different times and places, but never in just the same way. At that, social democratic ideology cannot be reduced to a 'pure' ideological essence. Its revisionist tendencies, flowing through the work of Bernstein, Crosland, Anthony Giddens, Maurice Glasman and others, speak to its unique political DNA. There is some truth to historian Tony Judt's claim that Western social democracy has been "a practice in lifelong search of its theory". Yet, that social democrats resisted the urge to offer, in the late scholar Lezsek Kołakowski's words, a "prescription for the total salvation of mankind", alerts us to its deeply philosophical nature. In other respects, it has long presented as a distinct ideology, and not simply as some pragmatic compromise between capitalism and socialism. Social democracy's syncretic tendency is in itself a unique political tradition: a hybrid of socialist, liberal and, to my mind, communitarian thought. Above all, its spirit is para-doxical: at once radical and conservative, romantic and rational, patriotic and internationalist.

This paradoxical spirit has been diluted as social democrats em-braced a newfound status as 'progressive parties' after the Cold War. Progressive parties talk the language of diversity, yet more and more they lace themselves in an ideological straitjacket. La-bor parties have always been home to people holding socially conservative views and have secured their votes. Indeed, as Mi-chael Easson has argued, there is a case to be made that there exists is a Burkean Australian Labor tradition.[120] Yet those of a conservative outlook or disposition are increasingly made to feel unwelcome in the party. Increasingly, there is only one permit-ted view within the Labor tent, and a licence is granted to per-secute heretics who do not subscribe. Yet as Pabst reminds us, the ALP is a party *of* the left but not exclusively *on* the left.[121] The most concerning development has been the embrace of identity politics by some within Labor (and among corporate elites) – the idea that we are all essentially defined by our membership of an intersecting set of categories based on gender or race etc.[122] This is playing out in devastating ways for social democrats. It is found in the 2018 ALP National Platform with its multitudi-nous LGBTQI references. (I was secretary of the National Poli-cy Forum which drafted the document in question, and accept responsibility for not speaking up during the drafting process). Blue Labour thinker Jonathan Rutherford gets to the heart of why identity politics is so harmful:

> Cosmopolitans believe that their obligations to others should not be confined to fellow national citizens, but extended to include all of humanity. Yet in committing to everyone as part of a universal humanity, we commit to no one and nothing in particular. Under the influence of this abstraction, progres-sive and left politics in the 1990s turned away from class poli-tics and solidarity in favour of group identities and self-reali-sation. It rejected forms of membership that make a claim on

people's loyalty. The particularist loyalties of the nation state and inherited national customs and traditions divided individuals from their shared humanity. Among the more radical, this repudiation extended to their own white English ethnicity. A mix of white guilt and post-colonial politics delegitimised English culture as imperialist and racist, and by default those who value it. The generation of 1968 created political movements around sexuality and gender and took up the issue of race, but the logic of cosmopolitan liberalism has turned identity politics into a competitive struggle of one group identity over another. In place of solidarities, there is a kind of Hobbesian war of all against all and a narcissistic preoccupation with the self. Everything is socially constructed, we are told, and so it can all be deconstructed and rebuilt in perfect order. In this utopian politics, the individual will is the guiding principle. Cosmopolitan liberalism has no account of what holds society together. Instead it reduces it to a collection of socially unattached individuals. Identity politics has become a modern-day substitute for the puritan's conscience. Like Christian in John Bunyan's *The Pilgrim's Progress*, a person can pursue "yonder shining light", free of the constraints of human association and obligations to others ... Cosmopolitan liberalism is the culture of the elites and is deeply divisive. Identity politics, in its libertarian pursuit of self-realisation and its judging and dividing into victim status hierarchies, is corrosive of society.[123]

The eminent left-wing historian, Sheri Berman, who is certainly not a Blue Labour thinker, has also written on the pitfalls of identity politics in the context of Trump:

Once the other party becomes an enemy rather than an opponent, winning becomes more important than the common good and compromise becomes an anathema. Such situations also promote emotional rather than rational evaluations of policies and evidence. Making matters worse, social scientists consistently find that the most committed partisans, those who are the angriest and have the most negative feelings towards out-groups, are the most politically engaged ... The short-term goal must be winning elections, and this means not helping Trump rile up his base by activating their sense of "threat" and inflaming the grievances and anger that lead them to rally

around him. This will require avoiding the type of 'identity politics' that stresses differences and creates a sense of "zero-sum"
competition between groups and instead emphasizing common values and interests."[124]

It is time for Laborites to rediscover the rich history of social
democratic ideas as a means of renewing a relevant Laborist
politics rooted within the traditions of the Australian way of life
– a dynamic, egalitarian social market economy underpinned
by a commitment to democracy and the common good,
whether locally and internationally. This entails embracing a
policy framework both social and democratic in that it doesn't
automatically look to the market or the State as the first solution
to a problem. It has the potential to tackle economic insecurity
and inequality at source. As a start, it demands Labor move
beyond statist progressive liberalism.

A note of caution should be struck here. Greatly exaggerated
predictions of social democracy's death have been made before.
For instance, during the 1920s and again during the 1940s,
communist parties emerged as serious rivals to western socialist
and centre-left parliamentary parties. During social democracy's
so-called golden age of the 1950s, conservative parties dominated
electorally in Australia and Britain. Many then argued that class-
based politics and associated social democratic nostrums were
irrelevant in an age of affluence. In the 1970s, critics again
predicted its imminent demise in the face of a resurgent centre-
right. On each occasion, social democratic parties revived, often
becoming a hegemonic force in key nations and, in Europe of the
1990s, most of the continent. The twenty-first century has raised
fresh questions about social democracy's viability. Scholars
such as John Keane argue that its travails cannot be separated
from the deeper crisis of democratic politics: a global trend of
declining trust in political institutions, parties and leaders and
voter disgust at the seeming inability of politics to tackle the
depredations of footloose finance capital.

Power and the labour interest

Politics is about power. Who gets what and how, how we reconcile divergent interests, in short how power is deployed, for better and worse. That struggle for power is as much a contest of storytelling as it is the cut and thrust of political debate in and outside of parliament. The best ideas – big or small – begin as stories. Sharing our stories and perspectives with one another translates our individual, family and community experiences – our thoughts, values, aspirations, fears and grievances – into the public sphere, where politics ultimately takes place. Storytelling and listening to those of others can help reconcile what Maurice Glasman describes as 'estranged interests'; it allows us to see our commonalities and differences, and to broker a Common Good.[125] A compelling political story helps avoid the tendency to prioritise tactics over a strategic long-game, in Australian Rules jargon, to focus on the ebb and flow of a four-quarter contest rather than a bone-jarring bump or spectacular mark. Labor has had many great storytellers over the years but now struggles to articulate what Glasman vividly describes as an "enchanted" story of our nation.[126]

Two stories, each possibly apocryphal, lead us to the essence of Australian Labor's foundational ideas.[127] 'My program! *Ten bob a day!*', a local worker is supposed to have told visiting Frenchman Albert Métin at the end of the nineteenth century when asked about his political program. One suspects that the interviewee was taking the piss in the finest Australian tradition – the labour movement's aspirations were never quite so narrow, as Métin himself knew. By dint of having imposed limits on the rights of property, established the eight hours' day, a minimum wage, compulsory arbitration, together with other measures the antipodes gained the title of "the workingman's paradise". Métin's thesis was that the Australian workman was a socialist without quite knowing it, "not because he believes in socialism as a theory, but because he believes that some of the results of which

are supposed to be due to socialism will do good to him individually." The distinction between theory and practice is drawn in
another place in Métin's work: "Australasia has not added much
to the study of social philosophy, but it has gone further than
any other country in the way of experiments."[128] Métin was right
and wrong. To quote Glasman, here is political ideology beginning with the world as it is, in which human nature is understood to be based on "self-interest broadly conceived", and "the
well-being of others is a condition of our own flourishing." In
other words, the preconditions of a good life.[129]

Our second story comes from an unlikely source, that of a so-
called Labor 'rat'. Saddled with debts, Labor MP Billy Hughes
hadn't expected an early election to be called in 1895 in the then
colony of NSW. His most faithful supporters were also caught
off guard. Three of them – giant Irish migrants he had organised
as wharfies but who now cut sugarcane in the colony's north
– journeyed back to Sydney as soon as they heard the news.
After listening to a campaign speech, the trio's spokesman ap-
proached Hughes and handed over a bankbook containing their
joint savings: £150, perhaps six months' wages for three labour-
ing men such as these. "If you get into parliament you can pay us
back when you're able. If not, it doesn't matter," he told Hughes.
Blinded by tears and unable to speak, Billy pressed the book
back into the hands of the man and ran for his tram. He was
re-elected with a whopping majority. Labor was created by the
likes of these Australians: workers who, as Hughes put it, "wanted to do something for others less fortunate than themselves, to
make the world a better place for men and women and children
to live in". They clearly also thought a Labor government might
provide a few more 'bob', a vision of self-interest conceived in
broad terms. It's the precondition of the good society. This is
Labor's reason for being. More than any 'ism', the good life and
good society are its animating ideas.

Some later commentators simplistically claim that Labor's mission has been merely to 'civilise capitalism'.[130] Their opponents on the left were wrong to claim Labor's mission in life equated to ushering in some abstract socialist society. Unquestionably, most early Laborites believed that their party would create a more civilised society than what had resulted from free markets and *were* influenced by socialism. Labor's early supporters also understood the party to be a means by which working men and women could themselves wield power over their lives and the places which they worked, lived and socialised. They saw their task as protecting hard-fought democratic liberties and freedoms won in colonial Australia. Laborism, more properly understood, is the strategy by which the labour interest seeks to wield power, power not as an end in itself, but the means to subject the economy to democratic forces – parliamentary action, robust unionism and by means of other self-governing, voluntary civil society associations, faith groups or otherwise. Whitlam was the last Labor leader to identify as a 'socialist', yet Labor's mission in the political life of our nation is the same as it was 128 years ago when the party was founded: to seek and wield power to ensure that all Australians are able to live long, fulfilling, good lives rich in meaning. This is Labor's true 'social'-ist objective. It's not rocket science. Yet re-engaging with that core purpose means hard thinking about where Labor has been and is heading.

1983 and all that

Central to this task is a more proper reckoning with Labor's '1983 and all that' moment.[131] According to legend, English teenagers possess a '1066 and all that' knowledge of their country's history. As the humorous book of the same name suggests, only two dates are remembered: Julius Caesar's arrival in 55BC and 1066's Battle of Hastings. Today's ALP also has a limited sense of its past: it's '1983 and all that'. Gough Whitlam's election in 1972, and Bob Hawke's eleven years later, signifies the alpha and omega of Labor history. In the Labor pantheon, Whitlam modernised the party upon becoming leader in 1967, both in terms of policy and personnel. The Hawke government implemented a less romantic if no less sweeping modernising economic reform agenda: floating the Australian dollar, deregulating the economy, and privatising government assets. But where Margaret Thatcher carried this out in the UK by attacking unions, Labor worked with them via the Accord and by implementing a 'social wage' (Medicare and superannuation). This is a simplistic sketch of those eras, but, by and large, it is the authorised version of the 'modernising' era of Labor history. To borrow a phrase from Glasman, Hawke Labor became the Platonic ideal of what a reformist Labor administration should look like.

Is it any wonder that the Rudd/Gillard governments, notwithstanding their flaws and divisions, failed to live up to those mythological standards? The nostalgia around the Hawke (and Keating) era subsequently became an increasingly repressive force upon Labor, weighing like a nightmare on the brains of living Laborites. Whitlam's reforms, and the Hawke/ Keating achievements in office which those reforms made possible, had deleterious long-term effects and are the source of many of the party's organisational, cultural and ideological problems. The party's relatively small active membership is unhealthily skewed towards the inner-city middle class. MPs are drawn from an ever-shrinking gene pool. The factional system has ossified into a tool of patronage rather than a dynamic source of policy tension and party management. Policymaking resides mostly with the parliamentary party. Aside from the influence of affiliated trade unions, Labor's links with working-class people are weak. The 2019 election revealed the party's widening disconnect from mainstream life.

Philosophically speaking, modern Labor places too much faith in the ability of markets, free or 'designed', and centralised government to solve society's problems. If, as the scholar James Frost puts it, liberal democracy requires a population who can both trust and *distrust* politicians and parties,[132] then so too Laborites should be more distrusting of the ability of government to engineer outcomes. Like many Western social democratic parties Labor has shrunk into a professionalised elite. In government it is often neither very democratic nor very social, but paternalistic and statist, doing politics to and for people but rarely with them. In short, Labor has embraced a bloodless form of statist social and economic liberalism at odds with its founding political purpose. Other possibilities are barely considered. This trend arguably began with Whitlam and which reached its statist zenith under Kevin Rudd Mark I. Similarly, Rudd's celebrity ways were a symptom and not the cause of Labor's chronic leadership instability and governing malaise. As a result, as we saw in Chapter Two, since Whitlam the party has increasingly looked to a Messiah for its salvation.

The '1983 and all that' school of Labor history is simplistic in other ways. As historians Paul Sendziuk and Frank Bongiorno have shown, when the AIDS crisis hit Australia during the 1980s, there were calls for the isolation of those with the disease. Hawke Government Heath Minister Neal Blewett stared down the fear-mongers.[133] Public information campaigns targeted the areas where gay men lived and socialised, and the community, rather than markets or the state, spread a message of mutual responsibility. AIDS was brought under control and Australia became a role model for other countries. Yet how many Labor politicians, unionists and rank-and-file member activists would identify this as a truly great Hawke Government legacy?

Asking why the Rudd/Gillard era and Shorten's quest for the Lodge ended in tears requires serious self-reflection. Between 2007 and 2013 Labor believed the GFC and climate change would play to its strengths, as it did in 2013-19 as regards inequality. Yet the 'debt and deficits' debate and immigration (2013) and fairness agenda paired with bold climate policy (2019) failed to resonate with enough voters in enough key seats. Yet the best place to begin the soul-searching is not 2013 or 2019 but 1983. Gough Whitlam said as much. Shortly before his death, in his foreword to Labor historian and commentator Troy Bramston's edited collection, *The Whitlam Legacy*, Whitlam wrote what he called a 'valedictory message' to the party he loves. He urged Labor to learn from both its successes and failures: to keep its "history relevant by constantly reviewing it, and revising it" in order to ensure its "contemporary relevance".[134]

None of this is to argue that the Hawke-Keating governments did not change Australia for the better – we are wealthier, more open and dynamic because of them. Rather, long-dead governments cannot write Labor's 2022 election policy manifesto – the mobile phone and internet-free era of 1983 is no longer a useful guide to our globalised world. Nor is this navel-gazing. We are still living with the consequences of the wasted years of Labor Opposition during the Howard era, when the party failed to reform its culture, think through its philosophical underpinnings, or map out a coherent, transformative agenda. The same is partially true of the era 2013-19. Labor needs to be more intellectually prepared for government next time, armed with an agenda capable of convincing Australians it can be trusted with making their lives better. This necessitates Labor looking further back in its history than Whitlam and Hawke and rediscovering its original purpose. Why? Because the last thirty years have eroded the basis of Laborism so much that we need to wage again the fundamental battle for the good life for working people that we thought, in the 1990s, had been won.

'those things that make life worth living'

Rediscovering Labor's lost traditions can help address that challenge. Instead of invoking a fabled Labor prime minister – Curtin, Chifley, Whitlam or Hawke – in order to espouse the essence of Labor's ideals, why not draw on the inspiration of the 'craft' unionists of the mid-nineteenth century? These men – yes virtually all men – sought to improve their lot without exclusive reference to the State. From the 1850s, following the lead of their British brethren, they tended to form small-scale, city-based craft unions representing skilled and semi-skilled workers in a particular trade. [135] Wages were a central concern. Their members came together for a simple reason: to improve their lot by increasing wages and lowering working hours. By cornering the market for skilled labour, for instance by excluding those who had not completed a proper apprenticeship in a relevant trade or instituting high membership fees, craft unions sought to force employers to pay a higher rate of pay than to lower-skilled non-unionists. Yet the unions they built from printers, carpenters, bootmakers, tailors, bakers, stonemasons and other trades aimed at much more. They promoted self-respect and dignity, and fostered trust and obligation among members. At a time when the welfare state was non-existent, craft unions acted as benefit societies providing workers and their families with a form of insurance in the event of accident, illness or unemployment. In the case of death, a craftsman avoided the ignominy of a pauper's burial. All achieved without the creation of a parliamentary working committee. They *were* interested in earning a 'bob' and restricting the reach of work into their lives, but as a popular ditty told it, it was a means to an end:

> Eight hours to work, eight hours to play,
>
> Eight hours to sleep, and eight bob a day.

In their desire to improve their lives and those of others, in evoking the basic parameters of a good life, these early unions foreshadowed the aims of the Labor Party that they would eventually help bring into being in conjunction with the so-called new unionists of the 1870s and 1880s – associations of industry-wide working people such as shearers, wharfies and miners – who were to follow in their footsteps.

Importantly, the labour movement wished to *conserve* as much as it hoped to bring about change, namely preserving the so-called 'workingman's paradise' of high wages and social mobility. Here it is important to understand the democratic tradition they inherited and built upon. Following the advent of responsible government and parliamentary democracy during the 1850s, albeit with a gender-limited suffrage, for most of the second half of the nineteenth century Australian workers and their leaders understood themselves to be a part of a democratic coalition, or a tradition of popular reformist radicalism, alongside small 'l' liberals, manufacturers, small farmers and other middle-class interest groups. They were 'the People', whom, it was widely believed, constituted both a democratic majority and overwhelming moral force for good, in contrast to the privileged 'classes' and greedy 'monopolists'. Australian visions of 'the People' drew upon and mirrored British Chartists and American artisan Republican ideas of the same period. Indeed, when Australian working men had won the right to the vote during the 1850s, their political demands, given their general ethnic background, mirrored the claims of the earlier British Chartists—manhood suffrage, abolition of a property qualification for parliamentarians, payment of members, equal electoral districts and the legal recognition of trade unions. There existed a belief that this coalition of interests had established Australia as a paradise on earth for ordinary working people and their families. Yet by the mid-to-late 1880s a belief that this achievement was under threat became more widely held.[136]

This much was suggested by the famous report of the Sydney-based Labor Defence Committee issued in the wake of the disastrous Maritime Strike of 1890. Only by forming a Labor party and securing representation in parliament it suggested: "can we begin to restore to the people the land of which they have been plundered, to absorb the monopolies which society at large has helped to create, and to ensure to every man, by the opportunity of fairly remunerated labour, a share in those things that make life worth living."[137] If you excuse the masculine language, pause over the last ten words in that extract: 'a share in those things that make life worth living'. There is Labor's mission spelled out right there. It's not as famous as Chifley's 'Light on the Hill', coined seventy years ago, but it should be. Its beauty is in the eye of the beholder. For some, it indicates equality while others might see it as an ode to equality of opportunity and what some call aspiration. Then there is the simple nod to the fundamental desire to lead a good life within the bounds of a common life: the reason why Labor was put on this earth.

Even then a closer inspection of Chifley's memorable speech reveals a vision of a party committed to the common good, a party geared towards progress not progressivism, and founded on a belief that material well-being is an essential precondition of leading a good life: "I try to think of the Labour movement, not as putting an extra sixpence into somebody's pocket, or making somebody Prime Minister or Premier, but as a movement bringing something better to the people, better standards of living, greater happiness to the mass of the people. We have a great objective – the light on the hill – which we aim to reach by working the betterment of mankind not only here but anywhere we may give a helping hand. If it were not for that, the Labour movement would not be worth fighting for." Most commentators and Laborites stop there. Yet Chifley went on to express something of the inherently conservative Labor disposition: "If the movement can make someone more comfortable, give to some father or mother a greater feeling of security for their children, a feeling that if a depression comes there will be work, that the government is striving its hardest to do its best, then the Labour movement will be completely justified."[138] Labor exists to conserve – working people's status, dignity and living standards – as much as it seeks to change the world. Jonathan Rutherford writing on the UK argues: "the Labour Party has embodied the paradox of being both radical and conservative, and so it has played a vital role both in maintaining the traditions of the country and shaping its modernity. These dispositions are not party political. They are qualities of mind and character that are woven into the fabric of our English culture."[139]

Chilfey's Light on the Hill is a classic expression of Australian Laborism, the idea that parliamentary action could, in tandem with strong unionism, civilise capitalism in the interests of workers and their families, through policies such as compulsory arbitration, tariff protection, until the 1960s by means of 'White Australia', and modest welfare initiatives. Yet the impetus behind Labor's formation was not confined to trade unionists. Socialism had flowered in 1880s in Australia. The Australian Socialist League first convened in Sydney during May 1887. Many of those in Australia attracted to these ideas were restless, intellectually ambitious young men who spent their working hours as clerks, shopkeepers and journalists. Leading members of the ASL included future Labor (Right) politicians such as Billy Hughes and William Holman. Yet socialism was adapted to Australian climes and given a populist flavouring. For example, the mateship of bush unionism was depicted as the salvation of toilers; in the words of the labour journalist William Lane, 'socialism' was simply the 'desire to be mates'. Mateship and the 'fair go' became the *lingua franca* of Australian social democracy. The intellectual vibrancy of early Labor is ripe for rediscovery in other ways. A handful of anarchists battled single-tax devotees and 'state socialists'. Monarchists brushed shoulders with firebrand republicans. Others owed their political education to Catholic Social Thought. Non-conformist Christian socialists abounded. For a time, it was possible to practice Methodism and Marxism.[140] Early Labor was a reformist coalition of actors and interests – a party of progress – a movement of men and women uniting to change and preserve their world. Yet in this they were as much radical as conservative. As Roger Scruton, a leading British conservative recently wrote: the "goal of our earthly life is not to remake the world but to belong to it."[141] This, too, is – and must be – the outlook of modern Labor, from the environment to workplace relations.

Writing in 1909, Labor MP and Australian Workers' Union co-founder William Spence argued that Labor's focus was "the bread and butter question", but he maintained his party was "dominated by two moral convictions: the Ethic of Usefulness and the Ethic of Fellowship". With Labor in power, Spence envisaged "an active and enlightened democracy".[142] Shorter working hours and better wages were not an end in of themselves but would allow workers and their families to participate in their communities, voluntary organisations and political debate – to be useful to themselves and others. Spence wanted to create a good life for all Australians based upon an ethical understanding that markets needed regulation but that governments could not solve all ills. Here is another reminder of what Laborism was really about: it was about taking the parliamentary road, and taking office, but was never limited to putting bums on seats in parliament, or upholding union rights, improving wages and conditions, or making provision for basic services and welfare. Laborism was a radically new idea of politics – social democracy. It was democratic in seeking to have the voice of working people, the majority of the population, represented in parliament and, in turn, subjecting the market to the force of democratic institutions, including self-governing unions. Needless to say, Labor rejected the revolutionary road and opposed communism. Revolution was seen as both a violation of tradition and a betrayal of the institutions labour helped build, to say nothing of the potential for state terror and oppression. But it was also an idea of the social – a 'social-ist' idea which had nothing to do with the means or ownership of production – of human freedom and liberty. Laborism held that individuals flourish within strong collectives – family, community and nation. It insisted working people were fundamentally different from other commodities, for they were not to be bought and sold on the market at any going rate. It is this moral understanding of material politics, as Spence shows, that underpins the Labor idea of a good life and good society.

Spence's story is worth re-telling at length as a reminder of Labor's past and pointer to its necessary future.[143] Spence was born in 1846 at Eday, one of the windswept Orkney Islands off Scotland. His family migrated to Australia when he was six, settling in the Victorian goldfields' town of Creswick early in 1853, where they briefly resided in a slab bark hut. By age 10, he had worked as a butcher's boy, shepherd and shearer; at 14, he held a 'Miner's Right' and was descending the pits. Wages for a miner in those days were irregular and like many of his ilk, Spence contracted silicosis ('miners' lung'), caused by dust from poorly ventilated shafts. Spence did not attend formal schooling and was largely self-educated; in his spare time he devoured the works of writers such as Blatchford, Ruskin, Carlyle, Morris, Bellamy, Marx, as well as the Gospels of the New Testament. It was here that Spence began a career devoted to improving the lives of working people through the building up of unionism, leading the influential Miners' Union and the Australian Workers' Union. Spence's unionism owed to a combination of nature and nurture. A concern for social justice imbibed from his religious upbringing, combined with first-hand experience of his father's stonemason trade, predisposed him to the workings of unionism. Equally, Spence's keen involvement in the rich associational culture of Victorian gold towns – organisations such as friendly and mutual improvement societies, debating clubs and progress associations as well as chapel life – meant that unionism was a natural extension of his practical commitment to the pursuit of the common good. He was deeply involved in the activities of his local community, serving as a borough councillor in Creswick and a justice of the peace, member of the local militia, and a leading temperance advocate. It is difficult to overstate the importance of Spence's faith. Spence was secretary of Creswick Presbyterian Church and its Sunday school superintendent, however he was perturbed by its perceived indifference to the plight of miners and also came to preach with the Primitive Methodists. Like many early labour leaders, Spence's faith-based activism was inseparable from his unionism, as he would declare in 1892: 'The New Unionism is simply the teachings of that greatest of all social reformers, Him of Nazareth, whom all must revere'.[144] When Spence suggested that 'unionism came to the Australian bushman as a religion', it was much more than a rhetorical flourish.

There is something of his contemporary Eduard Bernstein, too, in Spence's view of not confusing ends with movement-building means. As he wrote in his slim book, *The Lesson of History* published in 1908: "Our hope is in the masses, in government by self, and by everyone self-consciously taking an active part in the ruling of the collective life ... We have the power if we have the will. Let each remember that man has failed before because each carelessly left to some other the work of the Common Good. We must reverse that. Each must take his or her share ... the Common Good our aim, we will soon find common ground of agreement as to the way in which the goal should be reached. The best start we can give to our children is the certainty of better conditions; the sweetest memory of us to them the fact that we did so."[145] Two years later federal Labor became the first majority government of its type in the world. But would the religious Spence be welcome in today's movement? Or would Spence be perceived as some antediluvian throwback, a check on liberal progressivism?

We're not all liberals now

Liberalism is an important element of the Labor tradition, as leading federal MPs Andrew Leigh[146] and Chris Bowen[147] have each suggested in recent years. Indeed, Spence embodied something of the Australian tradition of working-class liberalism, of self-help, self-government and liberty revered by craft unionists. But liberalism was not and can never be Labor's defining creed. Laborism is not a project of abstract goals such as equality, diversity or various rights, in other words a technocratic vision of politics that has little to say about people's need to earn, belong, care for others and their desire for security. Liberalism has much to say about rights, but not enough of responsibility and virtue. Its proponents are wedded to delineating some neat divide between the individual and the collective. As a result, liberalism is less capable of conceptualising how democratic, self-governing institutions –

unions, for instance, but also potentially companies, mutuals, co-operatives and churches – are better able to constrain the power of the market *and* State, that is, forging a Common Good.

Largely speaking, of course, Labor has become a liberal party, a statist, progressive liberal party to be exact. The results of the 2019 election threw into stark relief this decades long drift. Electorates of lower-income and blue-collar workers, those more likely have higher unemployment and fewer migrants, and faith-based communities swung against Labor. Lower income voters actually feared a Labor government's impact on the economy and their (precarious) jobs, even when they weren't affected by its proposals on policies such as negative gearing. Swinging voters in low- and middle-income seats like Lindsay in Western Sydney and Herbert in Central Queensland voted to protect the franking credit rebates and superannuation tax concessions that flow over-whelmingly to the wealthy residents of wealthy blue-ribbon Liberal seats like Higgins, where Labor came closer to winning the blue-ribbon Liberal seat than it ever has before. To take another example, Grattan Institute research revealed that even though Labor promised a $4 billion childcare package, the top ten electorates across the country with the highest proportion of families using childcare swung against Labor. By contrast, the same work found that of the top twenty postcodes with the highest average franking credit claims – ones expected to swing against Labor on material grounds – only four had a two-party swing towards the Coalition. In a separate analysis, *Guardian Australia* journalist Nick Evershed found that voters who swung to Labor were more likely to have higher levels of education, were younger, and were people in work or study.[148] An ANU study conducted by Ben Phillips found a strong correlation with Christian religion and low-income voters swinging against Labor. Of the 30 most Christian electorates only two swung to Labor. Added to that older people are becoming a larger proportion of the electorate over time, and more and more voting for the Coalition. (Conversely, younger voters are ever more likely to support the Greens and Labor but cannot be guaranteed to stay there once they have families and purchase properties). Australia Election Study data underlines this point. In 2001, 19 per cent of voters were over 65. By the 2016 election, it had grown to 23 per cent. Furthermore, they have shown themselves as a group to be increasingly likely to vote against Labor. When John Howard won in 2001, 56 per cent of over-65s voted for the Coalition; 34 per cent voted Labor. By 2016, the percentage voting for the Coalition had grown marginally to 57 per cent. Labor's share fell dramatically, to just 28 per cent. The difference between the Coalition gain and the Labor loss reflects a general trend towards minor parties.[149] This isn't simply the story of wrong-headed policy or demographics but the alienating vibe of progressivism. Surely, doubling down on Labor's statist progressive liberalism is a dead-end?

How did we arrive here? It isn't saying much to assert that over the past fifty years politics across the West and elsewhere has witnessed the triumph of the 'twin' liberalisms. Beginning in the 1960s, the liberal left largely won the social/cultural argument. Society is more open, tolerant and permissive. From the 1980s onwards, the neo-liberal right triumphed on economic grounds. The market has largely usurped the interventionist state. The latter story is more complex in Australia where the Hawke-Keating Labor governments of the 1980s and 90s prevented the worst excesses of Thatcherism. The liberal ascendancy, however, transcends partisanship; modern Labor is, to borrow a phrase, a party equally fallen among liberals. What's wrong with liberalism, I hear you say? State socialism is dead, buried and cremated. So what if Francis Fukuyama was rather off the mark with his 'End of History' thesis? There is *no* viable alternative. But what if liberalism is not enough? Ultimately, economic and social liberalism champion negative liberty, privileging individual rights and personal autonomy over human relationships – whether family or community, and even those found in the workplace. Abstract values of freedom, choice and equality are preferred to notions of responsibility, duty and virtue. Neither variety of liberalism has very much to say about the people and places that we love: in other words, the essence of a good life and the foundations of a good society. But listen carefully and one can hear the liberal consensus cracking. Post-global financial crisis politics is stuck in a rut and we know it. The language of mainstream politics has a soporific effect. The spectre of a resurgent far-right politics haunts Europe. Having (mostly) swapped their jackboots for swanky suits, Greece's neo-Nazi Golden Dawn, Ukraine's Svoboda, France's National Front and Hungary's Jobbik represent serious threats to mainstream parties of the left and right. Charismatic populist anti-politics politicians are all the rage. In Europe, one thinks of UKIP's Nigel Farrage, new Conservative prime minister Boris Johnson, or the Italian comedian-cum-politician Beppe Grillo's Five Star Movement. And then there is US President Donald Trump. Australia has not been immune. In the case of Clive Palmer's UAP, it helped to deliver government to Scott Morrison. A non-progressive liberal strategy recently delivered results for a party of the left in Europe. Consult the case of the Danish Social Democrats who won the national elections in June 2019. Its leader Mette Frederiksen appealed to the working class by saying "you didn't leave us; we left you".[150] She won not by ditching core values but by returning to them, notably a sense of stability in relation to immigration and wages.

"Liberalism is alive", Maurice Glasman colourfully remarked at a 2013 think tank gathering, "and it is killing us".[151] Hyperbole of course, but Glasman is right – modern liberalism is not enough for Britain or Australia. This is where communitarianism offers much and where we might draw on one recent incarnation, Glasman's Blue Labour movement which arose out of British Labour's 2010 election defeat, and which in large part predicted the defeat of Ed Miliband's 'progressive' party in 2015 and the rolling crises produced by Brexit. Maurice Glasman is not a household name in Australia, despite visiting the country in 2013 and 2015. In Britain, the former academic, community organiser, and Labour life peer in the House of Lords, was for a time beginning in 2011 akin to a minor political rock star. A follower of Jewish tradition, Glasman's eclectic influences include Aristotle, Miles Davis, Lionel Messi, the Pope, and most importantly the Hungarian economist Karl Polanyi. Blue Labour emerged after British Labour's 2010 election defeat, in part as a reaction to Tory Prime Minister David Cameron's 'Big Society' vision. Highly critical of free-market globalisation and progressive statism, Glasman wants Labour to re-embrace a 'small-c conservative form' of what he calls 'socialism', one that places "family, faith and work at the heart of a new politics of reciprocity, mutuality and solidarity".

For Glasman, Labo(u)r politics begins from the assumption that the tendency of both the state and the market to treat human beings and the environment as commodities must be resisted. He believes that individuals flourish best when their lives are given meaning beyond the world of the market, or being told what to do by government, and are instead rooted in voluntary institutions such as unions and faith traditions. Attachment to place is central, what Glasman terms patriotism. The controversial starting point of Glasman's ideas is the golden era of British Labour. He argues that Clement Attlee's iconic post-1945 government built a bureaucratic Keynesian welfare state. That statist approach encouraged passivity and dependence rather than active citizenship. In the 1990s, Tony Blair's New Labour came to embrace the virtues of global capitalism and in its tax and spend agenda became preoccupied with abstract concepts such as 'fairness', leaving the voting public cold.[152] "Life", Glasman insists, "is about the people that you love and not about ends and ideals".[153] Labour should devote itself to strengthening the democratic fabric of society, certainly beyond that of Westminster, including the democratisation of its economic institutions.

Glasman advocates a new relationship-based politics, inspired by German social market ideas such as employee representation on company boards and stress on vocational education. These kinds of institutional arrangements along with regulation of entry

into the labour market, stress on regional banking, and investment in long-run profitable businesses, have made Germany's
economy dynamic and resilient, and its society more egalitarian and democratic. Whereas Australian manufacturing lies in
tatters having bled 150,000 jobs since 2000, Germany, which
actively supports such industries, is the world's third-largest
exporter. This is a high-skill, high-wage economy built upon
workers, companies and government taking a long-term view,
rather than chasing a quick buck or bashing unions for political gain. The great paradox is that the country with the greatest
degree of labour representation in its corporate structure, severe
regulation of the labour market, and the greatest constraints on
finance capital, is the most competitive within the international
economy. It does so because it is built on a recognition of a balance of interests, enshrined by economic democracy and corporate governance rules requiring shared financial information and
a negotiation of company strategy not exclusively set on terms
beneficial to owners and managers.[154]

Some caution is required. As Bongiorno notes of Blue Labour's
potential application to Australian shores, embracing anti-stat-
ism would cut against the grain of Labor's policy-making DNA,
something in existence long before Whitlam and reflected in the
Australian population's habit of looking to the State to assist and
protect them. Moreover, Blue Labour was a specifically British response to the global financial crisis. And post-World War Two
Germany did not develop social market institutions by accident.
Modell Deutschland is the result of a particular historical experience radically different from our own, namely fascism. Codetermination in Germany also arose as an alternative to the nation-
alisation of industry pursued in Britain in the context of the role
played by the occupying power, America.[155] Ironically, then, the
so-called German model was inspired by old-fashioned, hard-
nosed British Labourism and Catholic social teaching. This was
created from an unlikely combination of Ernest Bevin, the UK
Foreign Minister after the war, who was a former Secretary of the

Transport & General Workers' Union, and his allies in the British Trade Union Congress (TUC) who wanted to build up new German unions as a force against the re-emergence of Nazism, and the Church which preached the social utility of subsidiarity (decentralisation of power to the smallest, functioning group). British ideas of guild socialism, decentralisation, and worker participation were key tributaries fed into the German model which, of course, was also fashioned dynamically with local players and with the benefit of their experiences. Any Australian adoption of Blue Labourist ideas, therefore, will need to be calibrated with local circumstances. And Blue Labour's stress on association and non-state collective action also runs up against profound changes to the nature of society as it has evolved since World War Two. The techno-scientific revolution that spawned the internet and eroded geographically-fixed communities has fundamentally re-cast the *forms* by which we relate to one another.

In any case, communitarianism is perhaps a case of old wine in new bottles. It is to be found in the famous words of the Jewish religious leader, Hillel the Elder, who is associated with the development of the Mishnah and the Talmud. Hillel, a contemporary of Jesus, is famous for the saying: "If I am not for myself, who will be for me? And when I am for myself, what am 'I'?" In other words, Hillel was advocating communitarianism two millennia before it took hold of academia during the 1990s or figured in the triangulation strategies of left-of-centre parties. It's a view about how we best flourish as distinctive human beings, by being rooted in strong relationships; family, community and within cohesive nations. Communitarianism has in recent times also been dubbed 'post-liberalism'.[156] A wonkish term to be sure, but a word-idea with much to offer. Its ethos can be discerned in the post-Cold War 'Third Way' politics of social democrats such as Tony Blair, Gerhard Schroeder and even Bill Clinton. Some call it communitarianism rebooted. Postliberalism's central claims echo the ancient traditions of civic republicanism, elegantly re-stated of late by Philip Pettit's book *Just Freedom: A Moral Com-*

plex for a Complex World.

It is in post-global financial crisis Britain that postliberalism has generated most interest, attracting supporters from across the party-political divide, notably in Britain. Scholar and Anglican Theologian Philip Blond's 'Red Toryism' was one Conservative expression.[157] On the British Labour side, Glasman, thinkers like Jonathan Rutherford and Adrian Pabst, and MPs such as Jon Cruddas are best described as postliberals. A postliberal ethic is evident in the writings of former British Chief Rabbi Jonathan Sacks. Ex-Labor leader cum One Nation MP Mark Latham's once sat comfortably within the post-liberal tent before his decline into look-at-me populist antics.

What does post-liberalism have to say precisely? One high-profile advocate, David Goodhart, director of London's left-leaning Demos think-tank, writes in his influential essay 'A Postliberal Future?' that post-liberalism wants to fix the "unintended consequences of economic and social liberalism"[158] – the fact that despite being freer and richer, many of us seem to be less happy. Post-liberalism believes in individual rights and liberties but recognises that without secure, settled lives surrounded by love and recognition, occupied by purposeful activity, individuals cannot truly flourish as human beings. Stability, continuity and familiarity are instead its watchwords; a love of family, community and patriotism are not to be sneered at. Crucially, post-liberalism seeks to move the political debate beyond the individualist/collectivist dichotomy. People are seen at once as competitive and co-operative, as well as selfish and altruistic. "With their emphasis on freedom from constraint the two liberalisms have had too little to say about our dependence on each another", insists Goodhart. "They have taken for granted the glue that holds society together and have preferred regulations and targets to tending to the institutions that help to shape us."[159]

More controversially, Goodhart alleges that a gulf exists between 'elite' middle-class liberals and the post-liberal communitarian-ism of what he sees as the overwhelming majority of 'ordinary voters'. Clearly, Goodhart's essay is based upon the British experience, where Brexit and immigration are visceral political issues. And his proposals lack a thoroughgoing structural program for radical reform. Yet there are lessons for Australia, despite two decades of uninterrupted economic growth. And therein lies the rub. The triumph of liberalism has not necessarily made us happier. Witness the unprecedented reports of loneliness and depression, record rates of divorce and family breakdown. The implications of the 'ice' epidemic, especially in rural communities, have been devastating. Sociability and neighbourliness are in decline. Australians are less trusting of their fellow citizens but also more sceptical of the ability of government to deliver services or solve complex problems.

Nor have the twin liberalisms necessarily made the entire populace richer, certainly in relative terms, as we explored in Chapter One. Too much of our economic debate occurs in a moral vacuum. For example, productivity is talked about as an end in itself. There was something nihilistic about the manner in which the Tony Abbott-led government effectively killed off the nation's car manufacturing industry – as if we could not afford to consider the impact on individuals, families and communities of mass job losses and flow-on effects to the wider economy. One need only consult Labor speechwriter and historian Dennis Glover's arresting account of what happened to the suburb in which he grew up in, Doveton, in Melbourne's outer south east: multi-generational unemployment, substance abuse and high incarceration rates, and the physical decay of rundown schools and built environment.[160] It's much the same story which has played out in Broadmeadows, a suburb across town in Melbourne's west, Cessnock in NSW's Hunter Valley, the regional heart of Queensland, Townsville, Elizabeth in South Australia and the north eastern Tasmanian town of George Town. Consider the work of Kosmos Samaras, himself the product of a Greek working-class family from

'Broady'. Writing on the regional Victorian town of Morwell in Gippsland he notes: "In the 1980s Labor's primary vote in Morwell was around 60%; it's now 35%. During the 1990s, the Victorian state electricity industry was privatised by the Kennett Liberal-National government. 5000 jobs were lost in the region: 9% of the population left the area, including 15% of males between the ages of 25-44. Workers and their families that did not leave endured significant hardship."[161] The devastation of a good chunk of the Australian working class – what American writer JD Vance describes in *Hillbilly Elegy* as "haemorrhaging jobs and hope"[162] – has had a pronounced effect on blue-collar males. It isn't sexist or misogynist to point this out. One of Labor's brightest intellects Jennifer Rayner, who also worked as a Shorten advisor, has written of this trend:

> Between 2008 and 2017 the male participation rate in outback Queensland dropped by almost 19 percentage points, the biggest fall in the country. This means 5300 fewer men – about 20 per cent of the region's 2008 male workforce – were in work or looking for a job last year than a decade earlier. From abattoirs and mines, farms, trucking firms and processing plants across the outback, jobs have quietly been disappearing, often in their hundreds. Across the region's one-pub towns and stations stretching to the horizon, the jobs have gone and the men who used to fill them have stopped hoping for an alternative. The collapse in male participation in outback Queensland is an extreme example of something that is happening right across the country. As a share of the population, fewer men are participating in work than ever before. Thirty per cent of men aged 15 and over are now neither in work nor looking for it, this at a time when Australia has passed a quarter-century of uninterrupted economic growth.[163]

Wherever they reside, working people either blame Labor for their plight or believe Labor does not understand or care for them. These voters began leaving Labor in the 1990s and it is these voters and their children and grandchildren who have not returned. They no longer identify *as* Labor. Thus why the regions and suburbs swung against Labor and not the Coalition in 2019. They – we – are not 'liberated' by change, as Abbott judged of the end of automotive manufacturing, as many progressive liberal Laborites likewise hold. The more general trust deficit which has arisen in our polity falls hardest on Labor because its capacity to govern and reform depends on trust.

Ironically, as government retreats from the economy, power is increasingly centralised in Canberra – and it becomes even easier for vested interests to distort policy-making and even buy elections. Consider, here, the power wielded by major market players whether it is supermarket duopoly of Coles and Woolworths, or online leviathans Google and Amazon. Election-wise, Clive Palmer is estimated to have spent $60m with the precise aim of keeping Labor out. In short, we are witnessing the unprecedented concentration of power within both state and market. Bold thinking is required. The insights of post-liberalism provide answers to some of our nation's biggest, most pressing policy problems. Australian Labor must be its torchbearer.

Do not misunderstand my argument. The liberalisation of our society was generally a good thing. Few would want to turn the clock to an Australia of the six o'clock swill, inequality for women, ethnic minorities and gay people, cultural conformity and crude economic protectionism. There is no undoing globalisation. Nor is this an argument against the market economy or even a Trojan horse for attacking individual rights. As Goodhart suggests in relation to Britain: "Postliberalism is comfortable with the 'individualism plus rights' basis of modern politics but wants to balance it with ideas that mainstream liberalism has neglected: the value of stability and continuity in communities, character, the dignity of labour." It is simply time we take stock of decades of liberalisation. "The 1960s and the 1980s were not mistakes, they are just not enough. For the big questions in politics today are less about individual rights and more about the nature of our institutions and the quality of our relationships."[164]

Postliberalism clearly has its weak spots. Its focus, at least as seen in the work of Goodhart, on the evils of some tertiary-educated metropolitan liberal elite whose life-experiences and values are opposed by the silent, often-religious majority (or significant minority) is too simplistic in terms of the Australian experience. The tertiary-educated have families too and are burdened by many of the work/life pressures, notably the rise of the new precariat (to employ a phrase to denote those persons most at risk from economic and social insecurity), low wages growth and insecure work. Not all working-class people can be ascribed with a socially conservative worldview. In reality, most Australians are made up of a range of perspectives: small 'c' conservative, left-of-centre and other rich, diverse human values. This is the same category error made by the Australian Right with its self-serving, simplistic rhetoric of socially conservative 'battlers' being oppressed by progressive 'elites'. In any case, post-liberalism is not a monolithic creature. Among its adherents there are different emphases placed on rights and liberties, varying degrees of attachment to social conservatism, and divergent attitudes towards how much of the liberal project of the past few decades ought to be challenged or overturned.

How does post-liberalism operate in the real world of policy and politics? How can Labor adapt Blue Labourism to our local problems, drawing on our local traditions? The answer rests, in the main, in rejecting the idea of Labor as some 'progressive' party and returning to the central premises of Laborism: starting with people's basic concerns around family, work, community and country, and viewing the wielding of Labor power as a means of empowering people to lead a good life and build a good society. It is these basic ideas which Labor must again draw on to redefine Whitlam's 1969 'Party, Policy and People' mantra into a new, yet blue, agenda for party and nation.

6

PLAYING THE BLUES

There are some Laborites who believe that their party does not need to fundamentally change. They hail from both the party's left and right. In their view, Labor merely needs a more popular leader, its policy settings require the slightest tinkering here and there, its communication of those policies expressed in simpler but not radically different language. Labor needs to make the government *the* issue.

Such a response will not suffice. As a reminder, Labor has won one of the last nine federal elections (with one draw). By the time it gets another chance to break the drought, it will be close to fifteen years since it won a majority of seats. It has won government off the various incarnations of anti-Labor at an election just four times in the last hundred years and only three times since the end of the Second World War. Those three times, the leader (Whitlam, Hawke and Rudd) has been both more popular and more centrist than the party they led. Each leader's implicit bargain with the federal electorate was that they would control and moderate the party, they were in charge, and would govern for all. The same is arguably true of John Curtin's wartime leadership which resulted in Labor's greatest ever election victory in 1943. "Curtin today is wielding a big stick," wrote one sympathetic journalist in 1941 as Curtin imposed discipline on the hitherto unruly federal Labor caucus and the nation-at-large. "He is being as ruthless in his party as in Parliament."[165] The same is true of Andrew Fisher, the dour, teetotal Scot and fiscal hawk, who led federal Labor to victory and office at the 1910 election as the world's first majority Labor or socialist government and won office again in 1914. The brutal truth for true believers is that as far as the federal electorate is concerned Labor has had one very good government (Hawke) since the second world war and two (Curtin and Hawke) in a century.

The idea that modern Labor is in a prolonged crisis is not a newfangled view. The CFMEU's 2004 Brompton report published in the wake of that year's defeat argued: "There is a vast gulf between the beliefs and aspirations of working-class Australians — the type of workers our union represents — and the professional political class running the Labor Party. Until such time as the Labor Party machine realises that they have a fundamental disconnection with large sections of mainstream Australia, they will continue to face electoral isolation." "If they do not address this problem, Labor could face a period of opposition equivalent to the lost years of the 1950s and 60s."[166]

To put it another way, members of the Labor Party constitute 0.02 per cent of the Australian population. Taking out a Labor Party membership means one is not like other Australians. They do not share the true believer view of Labor or its centrality to Australian life, as great as its historical influence on our polity has been. Consult, for example, a survey published by the *Labor Herald* in 2015, the party's then official online newspaper. Of the issues members nominated for potential discussion with a shadow cabinet minister, the environment and climate change ranked first for 23 per cent of survey respondents. Next, on 16 per cent, came immigration and asylum seekers. The economy was seventh, attracting only 7 per cent. The budget interested just 5 per cent, and national security finished last with 1 per cent.[167] Laborites are the outsiders, the outliers, different to other Australians. Laborites need to better understand Australians, Australians in their fullest diversity, wherever they live – but Australians are under no obligation to understand Labor. If true believers don't realise this and put aside their biases and preferences and reconnect with everyday Australians, there will be no future for Labor. Indeed, if it wasn't for compulsory, preferential voting it would be in the position of its European comrades, polling far less than thirty per cent of the primary or less. Is the party up to it? Can it reform and renew its personnel and structure, policies and relationship with Australians (in Gough Whitlam's holy trinity, 'Party', 'Policy', 'People'). If it doesn't change, there is no guarantee of Labor returning to power federally, certainly not in the short-term.

**

Party

We begin with the party – its structures, culture and personnel. Australian Labor has been defined by its relationship with the union movement. The party was founded by working-class unionists, and unions continue to occupy a formal place in its structure as affiliated bodies. It is a rarity in this sense – most of the world manages to get by without such a party. Indeed, there are a handful of affluent, developed countries that do not boast any major party calling itself 'labor', 'social democratic' or 'socialist' – the United States is the most significant of them. The historian Robin Archer has argued, if the United States had followed Australian Labor's lead, it is "likely that business interests would have had less influence over public policy, that income and wealth would have been more equally distributed, that unions would have been stronger and that a more comprehensive welfare state would have developed."[168]

Since the 2000s, there have been increasing calls for 'party reform' under the guise of 'democratisation'.[169] Some point to Labor's national membership, which, having increased by some twenty per cent to around 55,000 members after the 2013 election defeat, has since plateaued. In response, there have been renewed calls to open up the party's decision-making to rank-and-file ALP members – and conversely remove power from so-called factional powerbrokers and unions and their elected leaders – in order to attract new members. Since September 2013 members have possessed an equal say in helping elect, alongside federal parliamentary caucus members (MPs), the federal leader. But the call for a direct say has extended to electing federal Senators and state-based Upper House members and even the introduction of an inexpensive 'supporter' category of membership which would provide voting rights in the manner of the British Labour Party. (US-style primaries, opening up the party's preselections to the public, have fallen by the wayside). In part this owes to factional rivalry, overlapping with a debate about the appropriate role of trade unions and union leaders in party matters. Most calls to democratise the party in these terms have come from a section of the party's Left, predominantly inner-city based and middle-class, which historically perform well in such ballots, and which is close to winning power in the party's major centres of power – its triennial national conference and powerful national executive. (Numbers are presently split evenly here, though Labor's leader, Anthony Albanese, who hails from the Left faction, exercises a casting vote).

Extreme caution is required. Firstly, boosting gross membership is a misleading aim. The challenge ought to be recruiting new members from working-class occupations, and from the 'new precariat', drawn largely but not exclusively from suburban and regional Australia, Labor's core voting blocks, rather than continue the middle-classing of the modern party. Left unchecked the continued middle-classing of Labor – first pointed out by scholars Andrew Scott and Michael Thompson in the 1990s – is a recipe for disaster. As Jonathan Rutherford observes of British Labour: "with the decline of the industrial working class and the growing influence of a professional middle class, Labour has lost its conservative disposition. Some will claim this is positive: the party is now more left-wing. But this misunderstands the nature of the change. Labour has become a more bourgeois liberal party, and it risks becoming a party in society but not of it."[170] Relatedly, the ALP has committed itself to a range of middle-class quotas in recent years – notably MP gender parity and on various other committees and the like – and made progress in this respect. That is to be welcomed and worn as a badge of pride. Less welcome are bizarre recent calls made by self-interested types for quotas based on sexual orientation and ethnicity. Indeed, as Michael Thompson points out in his recent book, *Labor's Forgotten People*, of the party reviews routinely staged since the 1964 'Wyndham' plan, the only substantive internal reform has been that pertaining to gender affirmative action.[171]

The ALP is in need of a new, meaningful quota system and affirmative action plan – based on class. Would former Labor Prime Minister Ben Chifley successfully contest preselection today? This is the counterfactual scenario party types routinely like to explore. A Bathurst-born engine-driver without a university degree stands no chance, some say. The ranks of modern-day Labor politicians are reserved for party officials and former staffers, full-time union officials and middle-class professionals such as lawyers. Others respond that a twenty-first century Chifley would in all likelihood prevail. Australia, they point out, is a vastly different place to that of the 1920s or 1970s. Bright working-class kids such as Chifley would typically progress to higher education, a virtually impossible path for their predecessors. As former ALP national secretary Tim Gartrell put it over a decade ago: would Ben Chifley have been a train driver today? Both responses contain elements of truth and yet each is flawed. Chifley's Australia is almost unrecognisable. The old industrial working-class continues to disappear before our eyes – even if class still matters. Our workplaces and parliaments are less blokey and more multi-cultural. The stereotype of the ex-Labor staffer or apparatchik with no "real" life experience, Gartrell says, is largely a figment of the fevered imagination of right-wingers keen to paint modern Labor as out-of-touch with the concerns of the battlers of mainstream Australia.[172]

There is no doubt that Labor's parliamentary ranks and membership have narrowed and are less reflective of the nation's occupational and geographical diversity. Few of the current parliamentary caucus toiled on the shop floor or hail from working-class stock or even enjoyed a career outside of politics, for that matter. This is not to say that ex-staffers, union officials and lawyers can't be good politicians. But their narrow career paths don't assist Labor's pitch to a working-class base. A case in point was the former federal Senator for Victoria and member of the Australian Motoring Enthusiast Party Ricky Muir.[173] Muir was regularly described as the accidental politician who landed in Canberra on the back on dodgy preference deals favouring a fringe right-wing party of rev-heads. Yet he defies easy characterisation: in many respects he is a working-class Labor politician drawn from central casting. Having not seen out high school, Muir mainly worked manual jobs – farming and in the manufacturing, timber and, of course, automobile industries. He has suffered anxiety-inducing periods of joblessness. In Muir's time as an East Gippsland–based forestry worker, he was a paid-up member of the Construction, Forestry, Mining and Energy Union. He was shop steward for the union's forestry division, which by definition entails a sizeable degree of activist zeal and concern for the wellbeing of one's fellow workers.

As a 33-year-old freshman politician his stellar maiden speech was punctuated by a passionate defence of working-class living standards, including the right to enjoy penalty rates. Muir, in short, is the archetypal Labor voter – a small 'c' conservative social democrat, although he would never be silly enough to use that phrase – his basic concerns revolve around the wellbeing of his family, his workmates and his community. So why wasn't rev-head Ricky ever one of Labor's preselected candidates or parliamentary representatives? For that matter, why wasn't he ever a member of the ALP? Tribalism played no part in his upbringing by apolitical struggle-street parents. Yet his failure to be recruited to the Labor cause starkly demonstrates the failings of the modern ALP. It is supremely difficult for workers operating outside the formal employ of the Labor machine and wider labour movement to actively involve themselves in party affairs, to say nothing of the challenges confronting an unemployed (or underemployed) person trying to support a family. Muir's lack of university education and high-powered university-sourced connections means that he and others fly under the radar of party preselection. Labor is the poorer for not having his ilk in parliament, yet I suspect only a minority of members would agree.

Historically, the best governments, especially Labor ones, were occupationally diverse.[174] Andrew Fisher's reformist 1910-13 administration boasted several miners (including Fisher), a US-born insurance salesman, a carpenter, hatter, engine drivers, journalists, wharfies and one half-blind ex-wrestler. The government's attorney-general, Billy Hughes, worked as a cook and general labourer before running a small mixed shop mending umbrellas. He qualified as a lawyer after entering parliament.

Bob Hawke's ministries of the mid-1980s included a doctor, shearer, farmer, policeman, academics, teachers, lawyers, a clerk (Hawke's Treasurer and successor Paul Keating), businessmen, a minister of religion, and an accountant. A POW of the Japanese during World War Two, Balmain-born Tom Uren enjoyed careers as a boxer, rugby player, supermarket manager and retailer. Whilst the government contained plenty of unionists, machine-men and lawyers, they were a diverse bunch of talented, driven men and women. And it showed. Whilst no one believes that Scott Morrison and Anthony Albanese are – or even should be – average Joes or Josephines, Australians like to identify with their political representatives, that is to see themselves as *represented* in *their* parliament. Therein lies the rub for the ALP. Its parliamentary ranks are unrepresentative of society at large. Given the nature of the modern workforce, it beggars belief that federal Labor's ranks contain no self-employed tradies. And where are the representatives from our burgeoning mining industry or IT workers, shop assistants, nurses, cleaners and small-business owners? Instead, Labor's parliamentary gene pool is dominated by ex-political staffers, union officials and lawyers. These folks aren't bad people, but their narrow life experiences are alienating large swathes of the electorate. Representativeness – the real diversity of working Australia – was once the raison d'être of Labor politics. Only worker-politicians, so the theory went, could be trusted to put the interests of their own ilk first. As the first proposal for a 'Labor' party put it at the Intercolonial Union Congress held in 1884, the workers "never can be as faithfully represented as by their own. Their opinions are only fully understood by constant, in fact, daily association; their needs can only be learned by the fullest expressions of fellow-feeling. Class questions require class knowledge to state them, and class sympathies to fight for them."

The ALP needs to be honest with itself: in important respects, the late 1960s Whitlamite party revolution went too far. That project was designed to make the working-class-dominated party more reflective of modern Australia. This was brilliantly achieved. Tertiary-educated, middle-class progressives in the mould of Whitlam were encouraged into both party and parliament. Which they did. The migration to Labor of the white-collar middle class set the stage for Labor to win seven of the next eleven federal elections.[175] Today, however, it is impossible for a blue- or even white-collar worker to rise up through the ranks: Labor is increasingly a party for but not made up of actual blue-collar and precariat workers. Making Labor a more representative outfit again will of course take time. It isn't difficult to predict that the forthcoming 2019 election review will embark upon a new campaign to recruit more rank and file members – by means of cheaper and online categories. Yet, as any ALP branch secretary will tell you, and for my sins I have taken on that thankless role, retaining, not attracting, members is the real problem. In any case, if it is to be worthy of the name Labor, the party must actively seek to recruit new members from the suburbs and regions of working Australia. The last thing Labor needs is thousands more inner-city-dwelling, middle-class professionals dominating its membership and potentially making up the next generation of MPs. Kos Samaras has explained the growing cultural gulf between working class Australians and Labor:

> federal Labor now largely expresses its values via a middle-class filter. The political party of the working class has not been run by train drivers and assembly line workers for over 60 years. You will need to travel back to the 1950s to find a federal Labor party that would look more at home in St Albans rather than North Fitzroy. Everyone joins political parties for very personal and just reasons. They do so to help elevate and advance issues important to them, issues shaped by their own values and upbringing. So there should be an expectation that middle-class political activists would join a political party to advance their issues and policies and if there is enough of them, as is the case within Labor, these policies will be pushed to the front of the queue. Their numbers are helped because joining a political party and giving up a lot of your time, actually costs you money ... political participation has become an extension of class privilege. In 2019 most (not all) working people don't have the money, time or want to join a political party. So what policies made it to the front of the queue? Free trade and the environment. Only the turnbacks issue would come close to soaking up nearly as much of federal Labor's internal policy debate airtime. Either at federal Labor's national conference, during countless media appearances, free trade and the environment would dominate how federal Labor would express itself to the country."[176]

Labor is as shockingly sclerotic as it was in the 1960s. It is hostile to new ideas and new people and stuck in a tired formula of policy announcements, speeches and talking head segments on Sky News or ABC. That just won't cut it anymore. The ALP can only revive if it opens up again to working people, becomes more dynamic, creative, idiosyncratic and democratic. Labor must take steps to reduce over-represented types in federal and state parliament. It must become less middle-class in structure, culture and outlook. If the ALP can enshrine an affirmative action quota of parliamentarians based upon gender, then it should also be able to cap the number of staffers, union officials and party apparatchiks currently winning preselections. Or at the very least demand that such figures spend a decent chunk of their working life outside of paid labour-movement positions before entering parliament. As a corollary the ALP should formally establish a new working-class quota system – a modest beginning might aim for twenty per cent of winnable seats. The aim should be to elect MPs without post-high school or tertiary education qualifications, or tertiary qualifications not acquired before age 25, and those who have worked in the workforce outside of politics.

Labor can also apply a neglected lesson from the Blue Labour experience in the UK. Community organising was absolutely central to the Blue Labour phenomenon. Glasman's platform (and his peerage) emerged directly from his record with London Citizens, and Blue Labour developed its first constituency in the party and among the media as a result of Citizens' (now Citizens UK) campaigns, such as pushing for a living wage in the capital. Organising embodies the Blue Labour idea of being 'radical and conservative', for example, faith-based organisations, many clearly not 'progressive', working in alliance with secular to achieve real social reform.

Labor should be looking to outside of parliament to effect meaningful change. Here it is worthwhile looking to the work of Arnie Graf, a community organiser who was trained by Saul Alinsky and in turn trained former US President Barack Obama.

For a short time, he worked for Ed Miliband's Labour Party. Graf drew on community organising principles to teach local Labour activists that organising people to work together for change means identifying what motivates people to act through identifying what they care about. No voter IDing, or asking strangers if they would vote the Labour program, but real conversations. Party branches will need to focus less on policy and ballots in favour of community campaigns. This real movement building will not only help Labor re-build concrete links with working-class communities, and pay attention to working-class issues, but has the potential to complement parliamentary activism and movement campaigns for social, industrial and political change. Most importantly, it can empower working-class communities to identify, foster and train leaders from within, who can in turn aspire to leadership positions within the labour movement. Otherwise Labor is asking working-class people to join a largely middle-class, secular entity where the rules and institutions – monthly, weeknight branch meetings exclude those with families – are stacked against them, or worse, they are made to feel like their views, and even presence is unwelcome.

Second, a party established by unions and mainly manual workers must necessarily ponder its policies, strategies, rules and structures at a time when unions represent a declining portion of the workforce, and manual, blue-collar workers have dwindled to a minority of employees.[177] Yet unions are fundamental to expressing the basic concerns and aspirations of working people and a renewed struggle against growing economic insecurity. Affiliated unions still supply much of Labor's financial support and wield fifty per cent of conference floor votes. Australia would be a different place without a union-affiliated party. This should give those arguing for seismic change to the party's historic structures moment to pause. Quite apart from valuable funds and organisational muscle, an army of unionist foot soldiers has always been essential to Laborite electioneering. When Labor emerged as a political force at the beginning of the twentieth century, its success was owed to the unions. Strong unions ensured Labor's survival across the century amid war, depression and Cold War politics. Labor's 2007 federal election victory owed much to the hard-slog of unionists in marginal seats campaigning against the deregulatory, anti-union 'Workchoices' legislation of the then Coalition government. As former adviser-cum-academic Trevor Cook notes: "The union relationship, at its best, gives the ALP a direct connection with thousands of activists, hundreds of community organisations and, potentially, millions of voters. Even in an era of professional politics ... this organic connection with the electorate can be highly potent." The trick is to make the Labor-union relationship work better for both sides. There must be a new emphasis on recruiting union members to the party who do not occupy paid positions within their unions.

Finally, the current 50/50 balance between MPs and members in electing the federal leader is appropriate: Labor would do well to avoid the destabilising situation whereby the leader did not enjoy the confidence of his or her parliamentary colleagues as per the British Labour example. In any case, a narrow focus on organisational 'reform' seems incongruent with the priorities of a party which didn't lose the 2019 election because of those links, and whose one majority government formed in 25 years, in 2007, owed much to the union movement. If the party wants to go down the path of the US Democrats then its proponents should be honest about the sort of party they wish to be members of, at a branch level or as parliamentary representatives.

Policy

Labor presented a suite of policies to the electorate in 2019. Critics have argued that there were too many policies on offer, which were often highly complex, and open to what eventuated as highly successful scare campaigns. Kim Carr is right in recently arguing that Labor cannot "just wipe the slate clean and start again".[178] Labor does not need less or more policy but better conceived and better communicated policies and more attuned politics. To be clear, I am not arguing for a small-target politics. There is scope for a more transformative agenda, moving beyond an obsession with 'tax and spend' politics and 'nudge' economics, the sort of 'we know what is best for you' statism lying behind calls for a sugar tax and the like. If Labor is more ideologically flexible there is reason for optimism. The trick is to understand the paradox of modern politics. As the 2012 European centre-left publication of *Policy Network* explains: "People want governments to protect them from the myriad insecurities created by globalisation and economic change, but they also want to be empowered with more choice and control in their lives, not centralised bureaucracy."[179] Labor governments exist to gain power in order to redistribute wealth *and* power, rather than expanding the state to redistribute wealth *without* power, and create rights-based legislation. Pulling back from of a statist form of progressive politics holds within it the promise of rebuilding public trust in social democratic institutions and may ease the pressure on Labor governments to live up to the hallowed standards of 1983 and all that.

Labor needs to break out of a policy vortex which looks exclusively to the State or leaves it to the market. The decentralisation of power should be Labor's watchword. (Both major parties need to tackle the tendency towards centralising decision-making power and resources in Canberra and, specifically, the Office of the Prime Minister.) Here it can take a leaf out of Whitlam's re-imagination of Labor's reason for being. He reframed the debate away from state versus private ownership and income redistribution towards service delivery and equality of opportunity. Hence the party's opposition to state aid for non-government schools was jettisoned. Whitlam insisted that Labor had to talk about more than industrial relations and focus on mainstream 'quality of life' concerns. Chief among such concerns was the shocking fact that in the 1970s swathes of

Australian suburbia still lacked proper sewerage facilities.

Pause over the term quality and Labor might well find its twenty-first century inspiration. What is needed is a focus on improving the quality of our institutions – from parliamentary chambers to our boardrooms, workplaces and elsewhere – while addressing economic insecurity and rebuilding shared cultural norms.

As suggested earlier, the key pillars of the Australian way of life – a fair day's pay for a fair day's work, equal opportunity for all and preventing excessive inequalities of wealth, status and power – are weakening. Yet these values remain integral to Australian's sense of our identity and maintaining a cohesive society and functioning economy. The ALP's election platform in 2019 spoke to the problem of low wage growth and economic insecurity but failed to frame the solutions to these problems in terms of a pro-business, pro-worker agenda, which brought Australians together. And yet Australians are keen to see more bipartisanship and co-operation, and not just in politics. To address the big challenges facing our country we need a workplace and corporate culture fit for purpose in the 2020s and 30s, and re-create a more resilient pro-business, pro-worker framework which prizes profit and productivity as much as co-operation and fairness. Stronger, more balanced institutions are needed to sustain a high-growth, high-skill and high-wage economy tailored towards the long-run, not one sustained by ephemeral mining and property booms, or which relies upon lazy, counter-productive measures such as cutting wages and making work insecure. To renew our national success story, and build a modern, thriving and diverse economy that creates and sustains well-paid, secure jobs in a globalised world, we must bring together business and labour. This is where Germany can be our Light on the Hill. Specifically, the German idea of co-determination can be the basis of the transformative politics required to reform our industrial and political life. It is the major policy change Labor should adopt to re-claim its role as the party of working people, economic growth, productivity and delivering a fair share of the good life.

Mitbestimmung. It's tricky to pronounce but this German word – translated as co-determination – is one law-makers and Australians should learn as we navigate today's policy challenges.[180] The post-1948 West German 'economic miracle' is a misnomer. Sustained German prosperity was not some accident, but the product of determined co-operation between government, business and workers. The centrepiece of its social market economy, the German Codetermination Act (*Mitbestimmungsgesetz*) of 1951, became part of its corporate furniture along with a legislated system of works councils (*Betriebsrat*) – the committees that can be formed to represent all employees at an enterprise level, which sees elected committees of workers informed or consulted on decisions concerning working conditions and rights. The co-determination principle is simple at heart: for the good of all, workers must have a fair say in the governance of the companies they make productive and profitable. Social market measures have been maintained by both sides of German politics and enjoy deep popular support. Whereas the last Liberal Prime Minister *not* to launch a royal commission into unions was Billy McMahon, German unions are not demonised to the same extent by conservatives. Social market measures were originally legislated by the conservative Christian Democratic government of Konrad Adenauer.

Whereas Australia has a unitary board structure, Germany possesses a two-tier company board system, made up of a supervisory board (*Aufsichtsrat*) and management board (*Vorstand*). (Most countries with co-determination laws have single-tier boards – notably Sweden and France). Co-determination is applied according to company size. The German One-Third Participation Act (*Drittelbeteiligungsgesetz*) allocates one-third of supervisory board seats to employee representatives in companies with between 500 and 2,000 employees. In Germany, a company with over 2000 employees ensures just under one half of the seats. Half of the supervisory board members of Germany's largest corporations – think Siemens, Bertelsmann, BMW and Daimler – are elected by their workers.[181] Having been elected by a combination of shareholders and workers, the supervisory board is responsible for overseeing the company's strategy. In Germany, the supervisory board's chair, who holds a casting vote, is always a shareholder representative. The supervisory board in turn is responsible for appointing the management board which oversees the company's day-to-day operations. The management board is required to have one worker representative (*Arbeitsdirektor*). While neither board can interfere with each other's operations, the genius is this – by virtue of employee representation management cannot ignore the interests of the workforce. In practice, the two boards typically work well together in a spirit of collaboration and consensus. At the shopfloor level, works councils are an effective tool. They enjoy veto power over certain management decisions pertaining to the company's treatment of individual employees, in particular redeployment and dismissal. Work councils possess 'co-decision rights' to meet with management to discuss company, finances, daily work schedules, scheduling of holidays and other matters. There are also 'information and consultation rights' as regards planning for the introduction of new technologies, mergers and layoffs. Importantly, they have access to information essential to bargaining negotiations, such as company profits and wages data.

The German model has worked successfully on a number of levels because it is a win-win outcome for labour and capital. Codetermination draws on the irreplaceable, shopfloor knowledge of a company's workforce and promotes cooperation between employees and managers. Workers have a better, more strategic say and employees receive a fairer distribution of profits by virtue of increased bargaining power of workers at the expense of owners. One study of 25 EU countries found that countries with stronger worker participation rights perform better in terms of productivity, R&D intensity, and had lower strike rates;[182] another examining the association between codetermination and inequality (measured using the Gini index)[183] in OECD countries discovered lower income inequality in countries with codetermination.[184]

In turn management gets a better sense of what actually works on the shopfloor. Works councils are associated with lower rates of absenteeism, more worker training, better handling of worker grievances and smoother implementation of health and safety standards. Conflict between management and workers is reduced and communication channels between each other are vastly improved. Directors are also drawn from a wider social and professional circle. All this promotes consensus, longer-term decision-making, making for better-paid, more productive and safer workplaces, reducing strikes, and improving the transparency of information such as salaries, all of which benefits investors, workers and consumers. This is a pro-business and pro-worker model that puts power directly in people's hands, because employee and employers are given incentives and empowered to shape *and* share the same long-term goals and policies. There is also less resistance to technological and structural change and greater flexibility in accepting retraining. By contrast, with the emergence of what is known as Industry 4.0,[185] Australia risks creating a technological-determinist dystopia unless issues of worker engagement are robustly addressed.

To take another example from Germany, consider this. During the twentieth century Germany transformed from coalmining to coal-machine design, development, production and export. Germany has just closed its last 'black' coal mine and plans to phase out all coal by 2038.[186] This is the direct result of codetermination, leading to superior environmental outcomes and technological innovation. Germany represents an actually existing 'just transition' – not empty, condescending rhetoric.

While Europe and much of the developed world has struggled to emerge from the shadows of the GFC, and Britain is convulsed by Brexit, the resilience of the German economy is striking. Germany emerged from recession with higher growth and lower levels of unemployment and youth unemployment. Germany has largely bucked the developed world trend of steady losses of well-paid blue-collar jobs to automation and to cheaper imports, notably from China.[187] German companies tend to invest for the long term, including in research and development and training, and enjoy large export surpluses and high output per head as a share of its economy.[188] Germany's manufacturing sector is twice the size of Britain's – 23 per cent of national GDP, compared with 11 per cent, according to the World Bank,[189] and dwarfs that of Australia, where its value-added proportion has fallen to 6.8 per cent.[190] In particular Germany's midsized manufacturers, known as the *Mittelstand*, are the backbone of the economy – their focus on innovation is vital to its success. A further comparison is instructive, the German steel industry has not buckled under the pressure of 'dumping' practices (in the context of international trade, selling exports below cost) by China.[191] German industrial giants such as Volkswagen are global leaders in their field. Thus though income inequality has increased in Germany over the past two decades, as it has in most developed economies, the increase has not been as pronounced as elsewhere.

This did not happen by accident. The case of Volkswagen is instructive. Britain's High Pay Centre issued a report on workers representation, which featured interviews with a number of German board members – both employee directors and shareholder representatives. During the financial crisis, a long-term perspective rather than the views of short-termist shareholders and managers ensured Volkswagen focused on protecting jobs, reaching an agreement with the workforce to reduce working hours, but avoiding layoffs. As the economy recovered, existing workers were able to increase their hours, saving the company money on training and recruitment costs. Excessive executive pay was also reined in. The supervisory board at Volkswagen secured a significant reduction in CEO Martin Winterkorn's pay package in 2013 after a public outcry. Instructively, the High Pay Centre report noted that interviewees from a management background were equally supportive of worker representation.[192]

Can co-determination work in Australia? This is to ask the wrong question; rather, how will our future economy function without this meaningful voice for working people? Employee representation would improve boardroom diversity by incorporating employee voices and raise profits through greater productivity and collaboration. It has the potential to promote better communication channels between all stakeholders; improve boardroom diversity by explicitly incorporating employee voices; raise profits through deeper and better collaboration resulting in greater productivity, better products and less strikes. As Professor Roy Green's work into High Performance Workplace demonstrates, Australia performs poorly in management capability, because of inadequate workplace collaboration.[193] Workers would enjoy higher wages and better, more secure working conditions. Co-determination might also militate against financial difficulties leading to the sudden collapse of firms, as has been the recent case with steelmaker Arrium and previously HIH and One-Tel, whereby employees and unions were blindsided through a lack of information. And it would prevent companies from disregarding their social responsibilities, for example the shameful conduct of James Hardie, which restructured its operations (and geographical base) in 2001 in order to avoid paying compensation to victims of exposure to asbestos products. This would benefit both employees and shareholders – the latter group were exposed to larger liabilities, falling profit rates and higher legal fees as a result of the company board's actions.

Finally, co-determination can help tackle the problem of excessive CEO pay. The 'two-strike' rule and shareholder pressure has not been able to restrain salaries that don't align with performance. These outcomes would each restore public trust in corporate Australia. While employee representatives on boards may slow decision-making processes, because more stakeholders are involved than just shareholders, the quality of decisions would improve and be tailored to the long-term. Co-determination could not alone increase profits, productivity and wages, and nor can it act to prevent all corporate acts of malfeasance, but it can create a more conducive culture. Critically, it entails not looking to the State to solve major problems. This is not mere theorising. One of the problems for Shorten in 2019 is that he wanted to talk about lifting wages, but governments don't set wages, businesses do, in tandem with benchmarks set by the FWC. The kind of economic reform we need now has to involve a richer and more diverse set of actors than traditional social democrats presently acknowledge. It's why co-determination must be the basis of a renewed, dynamic form of politics.

How specifically could the system be implemented? We already have a form of co-determination in place: superannuation where employee representatives sit on profit-for-members-only, industry fund trustee boards with employers. These funds have provided above average investment returns to members as well as investing in quality long-term infrastructure investments. Buttressed by industry funds Australia has built one of the largest and most productive pools of savings in the world in just a quarter of a century, and in turn superannuation has opened the door to a more secure, comfortable retirement to millions. One method of introducing employee representation on boards might be for government-owned entities such as Australia Post to lead by example. There is no reason that essential services such as water, gas and electricity companies could not be subject to a compulsory model of employee representation given that state governments currently appoint the directors to the boards of statutory authorities and government owned businesses. Monopolies such as public transport are also a logical testing ground. Wayne Swan has rightly argued that the Reserve Bank should again have ACTU representation at the board level.[194] More creative possibilities exist. Journalist Paul Sakkal has made the case for a form of supporter co-determination in our sporting codes, notably Australian Rules, based on the example of the Bundesliga, Germany's top-tier football competition.[195]

The question arises as to how private and public-listed companies might be encouraged to take up employee representation. As a first measure it is proposed that a business, labour and government roundtable be established to explore the possibilities of building a consensus workplace and corporate law fit for purpose in the twenty-first century and specifically consider employee representation. If consensus was reached this could serve as the basis of a mandate to create specific models of representation. It is recommended that two models be implemented for non-government owned entities with at least one elected employee representative sitting on the board of companies defined as 'large' according to Australian Tax Office guidelines (i.e. those with annual turnover greater than $250m): a) Compulsion, whereby Australian corporate law is altered to mandate employee representation. This could be based upon company size according to numbers of employees and/or annual turnover. This is perhaps the least feasible option. Or b) Voluntary, opt-in models contingent upon company size according to employee numbers or turnover. This is the most feasible model, which could be incentivised by offering highly-targeted tax concessions, vocational training subsidies or a phased-in lower corporate taxation for opt-in businesses. It could also be enabled by its allowance in industry-level bargaining agreements. Neither model would apply to small-sized businesses. Co-determination would be best implemented in Australia if accompanied by a more systematic establishment of enterprise-level networks of work councils.

Here, too, the opportunities arising out of such a system are beneficial to labour institutions. Worker representation is a perfect means of training future generations; the best, brightest and most passionate, schooled on the shopfloor and at work, in the boardroom. Codetermination is a bottom-up, nation-building institutional reform which can help grapple with the opportunities and challenges of the machine age, namely automation and artificial intelligence, and how we can make them work for working people. More than ever, Australia needs this change to bring this country together and drive the nation-building reforms needed for a new age of economic prosperity with fairness.

We need to radically rethink education policy.[196] Education was central to the agendas of our best nation-building governments. Think of the Labor governments of Curtin and Chifley that laid the groundwork for a near-three decades long economic boom after World War II. Comprehensive public schooling was pursued with vigour, tertiary education was expanded including the establishment of the Australian National University, as was a Commonwealth Reconstruction Training Scheme for returned servicemen and women. Robert Menzies' government pioneered the use of academically competitive commonwealth scholarships. In the 1970s and '80s, respectively, the Whitlam and Hawke-Keating Labor governments embarked on radical education reforms. Whitlam modernised education: the Australian Schools Commission formed in 1973 fulfilled Whitlam's vision of allocating funds across public and private sectors on a needs basis. University fees were scrapped. The Hawke and Keating governments oversaw a massive increase in the number of children completing Year 12. A more sustainable HECS loan system for university students was introduced from 1989. Yet for the past two decades our education debate has revolved around funding.

Australia needs a new education-driven policy settlement in the manner of our earlier bipartisanship, an education revolution, if you like, with quality at its core. The Commonwealth should take greater responsibility for the TAFE and vocational education sector, to restore its good name. Canberra can play a greater role by co-ordinating standards, sharing information, and funding in partnership with the states – an actually existing co-operative federalism. If, as frequently predicted, most jobs of the future don't exist, then these sectors will be at the frontline of our nation's economic planning, equipping new generations with the skills and training, and re-training the existing workforce, to fill the looming jobs void. Commonwealth leadership is necessary for several reasons: 1) we need a uniform national system of accredited courses with clearly enunciated goals like national standards around skill competencies and outcomes paired with a drastic increase to the volume and quality of vocational education and better regulation of entry into the labour market; 2) the distinction between university and vocational education is redundant and will be redundant to any innovative, job-creating prosperous economy of the twenty-first century. It's time for a complete rethink, which sees TAFE as an equally, if not more desirable, pathway towards a career as university. This is especially the case when the evidence shows that full-time employment for university graduates has dropped to 72.9 per cent. Doctors, lawyers and accountants, to name but a few vocations, only practice after completing an extended period of training and apprenticeship. Why not consider moving these vocations within the vocational education system? Moving such vocations out of the existing system might boost the prestige and funding of the non-university sectors, in turn smashing social class barriers; 3) in tandem with these Commonwealth-driven measures, it is time for the private sector to step up to the plate by creating vastly more subsided private sector apprenticeships. Employer groups and local chambers of commerce can play a critical role, acting as a conduit between government, TAFE and vocational education providers, unions and business. Such partnerships can better respond to immediate needs in the economy and workforce. Large companies in Australia, too, are often Registered Training Organisations such as transport and logistics company, Linfox. These institutional arrangements along with workers on boards and investment in long-run business strategy, make Germany's economy dynamic and resilient, and its society fairer. Whereas Australian manufacturing lies in tatters, the German powerhouse, with its immeasurably superior vocational education system and labour-market entry, is the world's third-largest exporter. The Light on the Hill – the lamp on young Australian's desks and toolkits – can be rekindled via the inspiration of Germany.

The previous recommendation does not mean to downplay the centrality of tertiary education. Indeed, one of the greatest initiatives of the Menzies government, aside from further driving Chifley Labor's expansion of tertiary education, was the introduction, from 1951, of Commonwealth teaching scholarships so that poor and working-class Australians could attend university in the first place. First envisaged by Chifley Labor in the mid-1940s, the quid pro quo of full-time Australian students having their first university degree tuition fees paid for by the Commonwealth and accorded a means-tested living allowance was the requirement to teach in public secondary schools for three to five years. More of the best and brightest working-class women and men entered university and, in combination with state-based teaching scholarships, bonded public school teachers enriched the classroom of the next generations. They should be restored on a merit, means-tested, bonded basis in the interests of our economy, social cohesion and secondary schooling standards, equity for low-income students, and a new spirit of reciprocity. While the HECS system inaugurated by the Hawke government has been a national success story, access to (and completion of) tertiary education is fraught with danger for working-class students and is increasingly out of reach. The priority of Commonwealth assistance to students lies with living and educational costs rather than tuition fees, in part a function of the HECS reform. No number of philanthropic schemes can plug the gap. In the same manner, no amount of increased funding to schools – government or non-government – can necessarily address teacher quality. A variation of bonded scholarships is currently used by the Commonwealth to address doctor shortages in rural areas via the Medical Rural Bonded Scholarship scheme. We need more of our best and brightest attending university and teaching, not simply as a means of earning an extra quid and enjoying a good life, but as a way of giving back to the community, improving educational outcomes, and forging a cross-class common good.

Outside of economics, Labor could think about devolving the control of services to allow families and communities a real say. Public education is ripe for devolution. Decision-making power ought to be more evenly spread, for instance board of management arrangements where a third of power resides with parents, so that the schools are genuinely places where they have power over the education for their children; a third with the teachers so that we can really honour the vocation and expertise of teachers, and then a third with the funder, government. The ultimate goal ought to be creating schools that are not merely tailored towards churning out more productive, high-income earning units – but yielding more rounded, resilient students and stronger, more cohesive communities. There is no reason why this logic should not apply to the childcare sector, aged care and various government services. The welfare state needs renovation. What is required is not a reduction or increase in welfare payments per se – though Newstart surely needs to be increased – but its wholesale decentralisation. Welfare policy should be conceived of and delivered with local expertise and knowledge in mind (and this especially applies to Aboriginal communities notably in remote areas). Welfare needs an increased sense of mutuality. 'Work for the dole' has a bad rap – the phrase itself was a poor start – but the central premise behind it, from a non-punitive point of view, upholds the inherent dignity of work. As Glasman has written: "All forms of meaningful human society are based on reciprocity."[197] Mutuality cuts both ways. The government's Centrelink robo-debt scheme, which uses a computer algorithm to identify overpayments, or 'debt', and which has driven people to take their lives, should be immediately disbanded.

Reciprocity involves trust. And we have seen how the relationship between politicians and voters has broken down. People don't trust what politicians claim or the statistics they use to make their argument. One glaring example is our national conversation about unemployment.[198] For too long front-page statistics – the ones that affect people's lives – have been hiding our real economic story. Consider the nation's headline statistic regarding who is looking for a job, the monthly and quarterly unemployment rate published by the Australian Bureau of Statistics. Recent ABS unemployment data is ostensibly good news. The December 2018 rate fell to 4.9 per cent, the lowest since June 2011, on the back of what some term a "buoyant jobs market". The unemployment rate crept back up to five per cent in the March 2019 quarter. ABS figures should be treated with caution; they are a 'survey' based on a sample of 50000. The long-term trend growth is geared towards the 'gig economy'. Less than half of workers hold a full-time job. Casuals, part-timers and contractors are on the rise – denied job security, sick leave, holiday pay, and superannuation – all on top of stagnant wages growth. The Uberisation of work can be discerned from other data. Total hours worked rose by 1.5 per cent in 2018. Yet hours worked per person declined. Under-employment – employees working but who would like to work more hours – is rising and reached 8.4 per cent in December. The under-utilisation rate — unemployment and under-employment combined — was steady at 13.3 per cent. The correlation between unemployment and under-employment – historically moving in tandem whereby the latter is two points higher than the former – is weakening. The differential is now about 3 per cent. As the *Guardian Australia* economics writer Greg Jericho warns, this indicates a permanent structural shift towards higher under-employment: bad for young or old, male or female. Youth unemployment is unacceptably high, especially in outer suburban and rural and regional areas.

There are three kinds of lies: lies, damned lies, and statistics. It's a familiar refrain. Yet people pay attention to the ABS's published unemployment data. Unemployment down is 'good news'; unemployment up, not so. How we measure and talk about unemployment matters. Yet many politicians, pundits and the public remain fixated on pure data, measured by a near 60-year-old International Labour Organisation standard – if you work for at least 'one hour' a week you are 'employed'. Granted, this data provides us with internationally comparative and historically trackable data. The ABS acknowledges one hour's work a week is 'insufficient to survive on'. Yet the idea that unemployment is five per cent and employment is equal to one hour's work is laughable. Real fake news. Our economy and society have changed dramatically since the 1960s. Yet the labour force statistics and the ways they are used by politicians and media haven't. ABS figures don't really take into account the increasing divergence between the new 'haves' and 'have nots' in the Australian economy. The 'haves' enjoy secure full-time employment and the financial and emotional benefits it brings; 'have nots' are subject to vagaries of insecure work, under-employment, and lower pay packets. Statistics matter in view of declining trust in our institutions. When the perception of reality on the street is so out of step with the Canberra beltway, cynicism and anger grows. It breeds the sort of nihilistic fury that saw Donald Trump elected.

It's time to talk honestly about unemployment data and insecure work, how we measure it, and whether it is fit-for-purpose in 2019. The one-hour-a-week definition of employment should be swept into the statistical bin of history. Any new definition of employment must be based on the ability of a citizen and her or his dependants to earn a 'living wage', not some outdated 'minimum wage'. Rather, it should be a version of our nation's famous 1907 Harvester judgment, that a 'fair and reasonable' wage must take into account the "normal needs of the average employee regarded as a human being living in a civilised community", crafted for the twenty-first century.

The idea of a living wage returned to the centre of national debate in 2019. In declaring this year's federal election to be a referendum on wages, Bill Shorten suggested that the minimum wage could be replaced by a living wage. Australia, of course, invented the concept of the living wage in the 1900s. In 1904 the *Conciliation and Arbitration Act* was passed. The centrepiece of the Act was the creation of a new Commonwealth Court of Conciliation and Arbitration to centrally fix wages and conditions. Then in 1907 came the Harvester judgment. The Arbitration Court's Justice H.B. Higgins determined, having recorded extensive testimonies from workers and their wives, that a "fair and reasonable" wage for an "unskilled" labourer must take into account the "normal needs of the average employee regarded as a human being living in a civilised community" rather than just company profits. Thus, the cost of housing, clothing, food and transport, as well as "moderate amusements" for a family of five living in "frugal comfort", were calculated into a basic wage. Granted, this living wage was imperfect. It was calculated only for working men whose dependants were assumed to be his wife and children. Single female workers, non-whites and Indigenous people were not covered by this innovative social policy.

Our workforce has changed dramatically over the past few decades – the idea of a sole male breadwinner is long dead, as are the industries that once sustained many jobs. Yet the idea of a living wage retains its powerful moral and economic force. A decent, civilised society cannot allow full-time workers to labour in poverty. A living wage is good for workers, business and the economy. It brings security and dignity to wage earners and their families. It can help stimulate consumer spending and address new concerns around mortgage and rental stress. Moreover, a living wage has the potential to improve labour productivity – more secure, satisfied workers will invariably contribute more to the firms they make profitable. How would a twenty-first century Australian living wage work? Currently, our minimum wage is set by the Fair Work Commission (FWC), according to five criteria laid out in the Fair Work Act's "minimum wages objective". In 2018, that was set at $719.20 per week (gross) calculated on a 38-hour week, or $18.93 per hour. The ACTU has pushed for a living wage pegged at 60 per cent of the median national wage. There is merit in this argument but perhaps a staggered introduction of a living wage – explicitly stipulating that the FWC set the minimum wage on the basis of "healthy living needs" in addition to macroeconomic conditions, productivity movements and existing cost of living measures – might see living wages average 60 per cent of the median wage over the medium-term of between three to five years. Alternatively, as an interim or permanent measure to achieve the same end, employers might be encouraged to pay a living wage outside of the FWC framework. Publicly registered living wage paying companies could be made eligible for targeted tax breaks. Whatever the precise method, Australia needs a more honest conversation over how we create, sustain and remunerate good jobs. It starts by putting the idea of a living wage at the heart of that debate.

We must radically rethink the way we talk about unemployment in other ways. Federal and state government must recommit to a genuine target of full employment. As a start, this means defining full employment simply. For economist Graham White it is the "absence of unemployment that is due to an insufficient number of jobs relative to jobseekers, including the absence of structural unemployment and underemployment."[199] Because what really matters from a macroeconomic perspective is how well we're using our labour supply. Full employment will necessitate targeted, large-scale nation-building infrastructure projects such as investment in renewable energy, tech-savvy manufacturing, combined with massive reinvestment in and quality improvements to our TAFE and vocational sectors. In terms of manufacturing its maybe a case of new wine in old bottles. There is a role here for the automotive industry which the Abbott government killed-off. As Kim Carr writes: "In the increasingly competitive global automotive market ... the advantage will not automatically go to manufacturers who pay the lowest wages. The advantage will go to manufacturers who have the design skills and technological capabilities to identify and satisfy the market's changing demands. Australia's automotive industry has those skills and capabilities, which is why the former motor vehicle producers are retaining design, engineering and test facilities in the country. Production of passenger cars has ceased, but Australia's automotive industry is not dead. It still has the potential to remain at the cutting edge of global advances in technology and product design, including electrification, light-weighting, gaseous fuels and telematics."[200]

Artificial intelligence properly managed, and with co-determination as its guiding star, offers hope too. There is the potential for entire new manufacturing sectors and corresponding jobs to be created right here in Australia. For example, the growth of the autonomous vehicle industry will require new levels of diagnostic skill, control mechanisms and maintenance, pit patrolling, and software engineering. These skills, and their emerging jobs, will require different education pathways for young Australians, and, if given the attention and focus required of developing new industries, could create a world-class intellectual export hub.[201]

One means of getting back to real full employment is the idea of a 'job guarantee', as developed by Australian Modern Monetary Theorist (MMT) Bill Mitchell and now championed by Bernie Sanders. This policy initiative aims to directly end involuntary unemployment and underemployment – to create full employment – which as its centrepiece would have the state hire those people willing and able to work as an employer of last resort, an idea which was familiar to Australians and their governments in colonial Australia.[202] This scheme is said to have particular relevance for jobs in the renewable energy sector, hence its association with the so-called 'Green New Deal'. This noble idea will be difficult to translate to Australia (and hasn't and likely won't happen in the US). "Our population density, geography, climate, and structure of employment and wage setting makes the importation of a US-style job guarantee a poor fit for the realisation of full employment," Emma Dawson recently argued. "Creating a pool of workers on one minimum wage, engaged in 'green jobs' such as land care, or aged and disability care, as advocated in the US, would undermine the award system". Rather she argues, a different approach to achieving full employment is available, best paired, in my view, with codetermination:

> By drawing on our own history of full employment policies and programs, in particular those of the post-WWII period resulting from the 1945 Curtin white paper on full employment, we can develop a multi-faceted solution to the loss of meaningful, secure and well-paid work in our regions and outer suburbs. This means not just an active fiscal policy, but the direct intervention of government in the labour market, through infrastructure investment, leveraging government procurement, revitalising industry policy, increasing support for research and development and – yes – even the direct creation of ... new, government-supported jobs in infrastructure, advanced manufacturing, renewable energy and other new and emerging industries which will require all levels of government and industry to cooperate across multiple policy settings.[203]

This kind of policy of course requires large sums of taxpayer monies to be spent.[204] The 2019 election once more exposed

Labor's trust deficit on debt and deficit. Labor's sums added up in 2019, it wasn't being fiscally dissolute, but a perception in the electorate of Labor not being able to manage money persists. Labor needs to reassert its economic credentials. Central to that task is Labor leading a mature national conversation about debt and deficit. Before the 2013 election Tony Abbott bemoaned what he called Labor's "debt and deficit disaster". In six years, however, the Coalition has doubled the nation's debt. Whereas most of the developed world increased their gross debt above 80 per cent of GDP during the GFC, Australia's ratio was just 16.8 per cent in 2013 when Labor left office. As of May 2019, the figure is 42 per cent. Australia's gross debt numbers $543 billion, up from $175 billion. The government's policy of banking extra revenue generated by the economy and offsetting all new spending with reductions elsewhere in the budget has been observed more in the breach. International comparisons underline its poor debt management: from 2013 onwards, governments have been steadily repaying debt. Germany's fell from 81 per cent to 63.9 per cent at year's end 2017. Ireland's debt is down from 120 per cent to 68 per cent. New Zealand's debt is down from 34 per cent to 31 per cent. Yet after six budgets we are worse off without any meaningful long-term investment in job-creating infrastructure, TAFE and more besides. To be sure, the Coalition displays a stubborn unwillingness to address debt. It continues to shirk serious, structural repair such as fixing capital gains tax and negative gearing distortions on the revenue side, to say nothing of taking a tough approach to tax avoidance by giant multinationals and big business.

Labor can draw a contrast between itself and a cash-splashing Coalition through introduction of a National Debt Commission. There is of course no substitute for government setting priorities, yet such a commission could be bipartisan and composed of people like former Liberal leader John Hewson, former Labor prime minister Paul Keating, former Reserve Bank governor Glenn Stevens, and ex-ACTU secretary Bill Kelty. Business figures like Heather Ridout, Janine Allis or Naomi Simson spring to mind. The NDC should take submissions from businesses of all shapes and sizes, unions, academics, entrepreneurs, civil society organisations, state and local governments; in short, the entire spectrum of Australian life. It should be tasked with making recommendations on budget repair and debt reduction that are fair, credible and do not place a disproportionate amount of the burden on working Australians, young or old, or our most vulnerable. The Australian public are weary of slick words and tricks, accompanied by glittering baubles at election time. They know they'll be the ones left paying the bill. Voters are smarter and more conscientious than their leaders often give them credit for. We need national leaders who take the country into their confidence and chart a sensible, sustainable course for Australia's future.

***

Democracy for all

Clive Palmer's outrageous election-year-long advertisements claiming Labor was selling the country to China were an unmitigated lie which pandered to xenophobia. Yet they resonated for a reason. When the public sees current and ex-Labor MPs kowtowing to the Communist Chinese Party government, they take notice. When they hear Laborites parroting CCP propaganda and historical revisionism, they mark Labor down. They are less trusting of Labor to protect them and their loved ones and their democratic freedoms. This is not about the Chinese people, it is about a one-party state which is spreading its anti-democratic ideas globally. It is contemptuous of democracy, of the rule of law, and Australian traditions like free trade unions. The systematic oppression of China's Uighur Muslim minority recalls the Soviet Union's Gulag Archipelago. As I write, the brave citizens of Hong Kong are rising-up against Beijing-led interference.

Emphasising the 'democratic' in 'social democratic' is not a newfangled idea. "I am a democrat first, and then a socialist", announced E.J. Russell a Labor Senator elected to parliament in 1906. "I am a straight-out Laborite, prepared to proceed on Socialistic lines only as far as the people's education will allow them to go".[205] And yet the undermining of democracy, as we have witnessed with Russian interference in the 2016 US Presidential elections, is not confined to local revolutionaries of left or right. "To be corrupted by totalitarianism one does not have to live in a totalitarian country. The mere prevalence of certain ideas can spread a kind of poison that makes one subject after another impossible ..."[206] So wrote the great anti-totalitarian polemicist George Orwell in 1946. Three decades on from the end of the Cold War, authoritarianism, whether soft or hard, is on the rise globally. Russia, Turkey and China and its leaders Vladimir Putin, Recep Erdogan and Xi Jinping are the most prominent faces of this club of strongmen leaders. The spectre of a resurgent far-right politics haunts Europe. Charismatic alt-right politicians are all the rage. Far-left demagogues are challenging the leadership of social democratic parties or superseding them altogether.

Granted, the majority of the world's countries are governed by democratic regimes. But the percentage of the globe's population living under autocratic rule hovers around four billion. Still, for some pundits and, shamefully, a handful of Laborites, democracy has become an intellectual fashion accessory, a luxury Gucci bag good enough for the citizens of the West but optional for the rest. Labor in Opposition and the next Labor government must take an unequivocal stand on behalf of democracy in our region and the world over, no matter the noise generated by deeply compromised figures from both major political parties.

Which brings us to the long-running debate over Australia's approach to the rise of China, and more recently, discussion around restoring real involvement with the Quadrilateral Security Dialogue with the US, India and Japan, or so-called

'Quad'. The Quad is demonstrably in Australia's interest, contrary to the claims of the Beijing 'right or wrong' lobby. It is not a form of US containment or tantamount to a formal military alliance. Australia's involvement would not be acting contrary to its own interests, namely ignoring predictions that China's economy will be double the size of the American economy in twenty years' time. Responding to the challenge of China's rise does not offer a simple 'either or' choice. No serious leader or serious observer has ever argued as such. It is the inarguable basis of any realistic and well-balanced Australian foreign policy. The great democratic challenge of our time is reconciling the demands of Australia's important economic relationship with China, our largest trading partner, with our legitimate national security needs and relationship with the US, our largest strategic ally, one predicated on a joint, unshakeable commitment to democracy. It entails not ignoring China's military build-up in the South China Sea. Or the plight of the Uighurs. It demands we speak out against the threat of North Korea and China's crucial role on the Korean peninsula. It cannot mean uncritical support for Beijing's Belt and Road initiative. Must we not be seen in company of democratic friends at the risk of causing imagined offence? Or is this the new orthodoxy, whereby Australian support for democratic principles and alliances is of itself unfashionable? Orwell knew a thing or two about such matters. The unwavering social democrat paid a price for opposing Stalin's regime, and contesting the naïve argument that the Soviet Union was the major opponent of Nazism: namely, unemployment and exile from Britain's literary class. John Curtin paid a higher price. His wartime sacrifice sent him to an early grave in 1945, the year Orwell began penning his classic work. Our nation's future depends upon navigating our relationship with modern China, but it cannot be pursued at the cost of betraying Labor's democratic and internationalist traditions.

**

People

Culture and language are important. As Chapter Five argued Labor has not and should not be some straight-forwardly 'progressive' party. Labor is a Labor Party. It's in the name. 'Labor'. A party of the labour interest, by the labour interest, and for the labour interest. This does not mean it is an exclusively union-based party or only concerned with work, wages and the regulation of work. And being the party of the labour interest is not incongruent with aspiring to be a party of government for all Australians, acting in the national interest, seeking to broker a Common Good. But if a majority of Labor MPs and members believe that Labor is a 'progressive' party, then they need to be honest and brave enough to seek to rename the party as such. As such, the Australian Labor Party can become the Australian Progressive Party or the Australian Progressives. Proponents of change might, if they wish, point to the various anti-Labor incarnations which have seen Labor's opponents variously called free-trade, protectionist, Fusion, the Commonwealth Liberal Party, Nationalists, the United Australia Party and finally the Liberal Party of Australia. The Nationals, of course, were once called the Country Party. And, after all, the first Victorian Labor Party was called the Progressive Political League (circa 1891). Then again, if Labor's progressives don't or can't make the case for change there is another alternative: cease referring to Labor as a progressive (or liberal) party and its aims and policies as progressive. After all, we might estimate that perhaps fifteen to twenty per cent of the population expressly identify as 'progressive'. To cast one's party in this mould then, would, to most reasonable observers, potentially alienate eighty per cent of the electorate.

This is not an argument for Labor to focus exclusively its policy attentions and messaging to blue-collar workers, or socially conservative voters, though they sorely need more attention. Rather in the nation-building Laborist tradition of prime ministers such as Fisher, Hawke, Whitlam and Hawke, the party needs to draw together what Pabst calls the "overlapping material interests and immaterial values" of working and middle-class Australians. "They will vote for a party that offers a sense of common purpose to achieve a transformative agenda, matched by a sense of mutual obligations to deliver it. Both parts of Australian society are attached to their individual rights and freedoms, but they also accept and cherish the fact that they have duties to others – to their families, neighbours, colleagues, and fellow citizens."[207]

Labor, to that end, needs unashamedly to re-embrace the language of patriotism, understood of as a dignified pride in one's country and a desire to make it better. It means more than being trusted with national security, as important as that subject is. A robust Labor patriotism – what the former Human Rights Commissioner Tim Soutphommasane terms 'progressive patriotism' – can mobilise voters emotionally, bind them together in a common project, maintain our historically high rates of social cohesion, and preserve Australia's attachment to economic egalitarianism and social solidarity. As Soutphommasane argues of patriotism: "it is no different to other forms of loyalty or love, and a necessary condition of collective self-improvement."[208]

A patriotism of progress, call it progressive patriotism, once hallmarked Australian Labor, albeit frequently paired with the party's fervent pre-1960s support for the racially discriminatory White Australia policy. In 1894, when the Shearers' Union and the General Labourers' Union merged, its members decided to call the new organisation, the Australian Workers' Union. The choice of the word 'Australia' would, according to one of the union's co-founders, Arthur Rae, writing under the pseudonym 'Hank Morgan', express "something real, comprehensive, and national", appealing to the "common-sense, the sympathies and the patriotism of everyone who is either a native born or adopted citizen of this great land." "[T]he word 'Workers'" ... is pure plain English and includes every class of Labor which can minister to the comforts, the necessities, or the legitimate amusement of the people."[209]

When the Australian two-party system emerged in 1909, Labor was the party of progressive nationalism; strong on defence and nation-building yet loyal to the British Empire. An oft-repeated boast was that Labor constituted the only 'real' national party in Australia. A writer of the Victorian *Labor Call* newspaper argued as such: 'The Conservative Press is in the habit of alluding to the Labor Party as the misnamed party. This, in a sense, is true: it should be the Progressive National Party."[210] Other symbolic declarations defined Labor as the party of Australian patriotism. At the 1908 federal ALP conference the workers' party took on the title of the *Australian* Labor Party, distinguishing itself from other members of the Socialist International. In 1910, the first Labor Speaker, Charlie MacDonald in the House of Representatives, and Joseph Turley, the first Labor President of the Senate, dispensed with the British-style wigs and gowns which Labor Senator Thomas Givens had described as "ridiculous flummery".[211] Later that same year its Postmaster General, George Pearce, introduced the first Commonwealth uniform penny postage, insisting that the King's image be replaced with the kangaroo on a map of Australia. The first Fisher government practically established the national capital. Labor's emphasis on its patriotic credentials reflected the heartfelt beliefs of its members but was also an electoral strategy designed to deflect criticism that it was a sectional party of the inner-city, unionised working class. To win take office, city and rural marginal seats would have to be won. Labor's message needed to be preached beyond the already converted. WA Woods described Labor's platform with a view to luring such supporters: "Embodied in its various planks would be found the noblest aims and highest ideals of true Australianism ... which made for the prosperity and well-being of the whole community."[212] In 1910, Labor swept into majority government, a world for a party of type – its status as the party of patriotic progress had done it no harm.

World War One witnessed Labor split over conscription for overseas service in 1916.[213] Subsequently the Labor leadership and its rank-and-file lurched leftwards, confirmed by the revised ALP objective adopted in 1919. The "cultivation of an Australian sentiment" was joined by declarations of international solidarity and explicitly socialist and anti-war objectives. Hitherto the champion of Australian nationalism, Labor now looked to inspiration offshore, as per the 1917 Russian Revolution. And although most remained committed to the parliamentary path to socialism, leading activists delighted in proclaiming the emergence of a 'new' Labor party. The electorate was rather less pleased. In April 1916 all but Victoria was Labor governed; in 1918 only Queensland remained. Federal Labor proceeded to lose five elections on the trot. (The state-based recovery was speedier.) Neither the war nor the further calamitous splits Labor suffered expunged the party's hope in the power of parliamentary democracy and egalitarian nation-building as a means of civilising capitalism. In 1918 the then editor of the *Westralian Worker* newspaper John Curtin lashed "hypocritical" capitalists who supported the conscription of life but were not prepared to "lay their worldly possessions upon the altar of nation."[214] And it would be Curtin whose World War Two prime ministership won back the mantle of patriotism. When Curtin opened the Australian War Memorial at Canberra in 1941, he declared it "would give continuity to the Anzac tradition and the basic impulses of the nation." "To-day, as in 1915, men are dying so that the nation may live ... To the men placing their very lives on the altar of the nation's hopes as they take their place in the front rank of our fighting forces, to the men and women working long hours in the munition factories and essential industries, to all of you, I say: This Anzac spirit, this spirit of Gallipoli and Tobruk, will be our inspiration. We will resolve, each and every one of us, to work and fight, putting all else aside, so that

Australia shall be the forever the home of the Anzac people."[215]

It is no surprise that the best Labor prime minister after Curtin, Hawke, naturally gravitated towards the language of patriotism, to tell an enchanted story of the Australian people, of what distinguished us as a people and bound us together, albeit shorn of its earlier racism and British race patriotism. His 1983 election motto, 'Bringing Australia Together' encapsulated his nationalist-accented consensus politics. Economically speaking, this call to arms manifested itself in the Accord between the government and the ACTU. Ironically, Hawke, despite his ocker image, didn't seek to impose a uniform national character on to modern Australia. Inclusiveness was his watch word. "None of us is entitled to claim real 'Australianness' on the basis of ancestry alone", he declared in a speech on Australia Day 1988. Praising Australia's multicultural diversity, he said that to be an Australian was simply to have a commitment to Australia. At Gallipoli in 1990, Hawke delivered a speech on the 75th anniversary of the landings. He lauded mateship as the Australian people's "self-recognition of their dependence upon one another". Hawke noted that the men at Gallipoli had been drawn from every walk of life and different backgrounds before being "cast upon these hostile shores, 12,000 miles from home". Hawke argued that 'there lay the genesis of the Anzac tradition'. "It was a simple but deep commitment to one another, each to his fellow Australian ... It is that commitment, now as much as ever — now, with all the vast changes occurring in our nation, more than ever — it is that commitment to Australia, which defines, and alone defines, what is to be an Australian. The commitment is all." Hawke's nationalist fluency did little harm to his electoral prospects. Labor won an unprecedented four elections on the trot: 1983, 1984, 1987, and 1990, albeit each subsequent election from the first with an alarming decline in Labor's primary vote. Such was Hawke's identification with the national zeitgeist, according to a poll conducted in 1988, his ambitious treasurer, Paul Keating, wasn't regarded as serious prime-ministerial material, because he lacked the "mateship factor".[216] Hawke was able to manage change while speaking to the continuity of national values.

In 2019, a Laborite patriotism means talking about what we need to preserve in our national life as much as what we need to change. Addressing the University of Melbourne's Economic and Social Outlook conference, Bill Shorten seemed to capture that very idea. He declared himself to be a reformer "because I believe in the things that have to be done to make people's lives better." Yet he also told a room filled with the high-priests of liberalism that he was a "conserver — a conserver because I want to save what is great about our nation."[217] The public need to hear far more from Labor people about what makes Australia tick, its achievements as much as its failings, and the shared values and common culture that binds us together, and of how Labor is intrinsically tied to the Australian way of life we take for granted. Yes, that includes expressing pride in migration, and ethnic and religious diversity. Yes, it means recognising our First Australians in our constitution. The Uluru Statement should be embraced. It is not some post-material obsession of the Left: it matters not only in its own right, in terms of social justice, but also in terms of the moral and international standing of Australia under any government. And yes, it means advocating for an Australian Republic. Leading Labor thinker, speechwriter and former head of the Australian Republican Movement, Michael Cooney, puts the case thus:

> ... winning a campaign for constitutional change has to be a campaign which persuades the nation, not a section. Persuading Australians to make the change to an Australian head of state requires persuading Australians outside the Labor tribe. The argument for an Australian head of state can't rely only on the traditional elements that sound right and feel good on the inside. Rather, the republican argument has to embrace prudent conservative patriots who have perhaps long been more persuaded by the idea of an Australian republic than by the republican movement. This is essential to building bipartisan leadership which will enable the question

to be put, but it's not the hard bit. The hard bit is reaching people who identify neither as Labor or Liberal, but simply as Australians, unattached to the parties and unenchanted by the leaders.[218]

All of this, however, entails reworking a Labor story which places family, work and community at the heart of Labor's idea of this nation of 25 million souls; its story of the good life, of the good society and the common good. Anthony Albanese, speaking to the Labor caucus in the heady first days of his leadership, described the Labor mission in these terms: Australians deserve the "opportunity to aspire to a better life. But it's not just about individualism, because I believe Australians firmly want not just a better life for themselves, they want a better life for their family, they want a better life for their neighbours, they want a better life for their community and for their nation. And that's what Labor offers. That's what we need to clearly articulate."[219]

Finally, a word on Albanese's ostensible factional opponents: the Labor Right, my faction.[220] It has gradually lost its way after the Cold War's end. The Right's modus operandi had rested in part on keeping the Left, apologists for communism in their view, at least in NSW, away from the levers of power. Significant too was the decline of Catholicism as an animating political force in the lives of Right figures. Faith was an important glue – along with unionism and even football club membership – that held Labor Right activists together. If the Right fails to coalesce around a new agenda – modernising and traditionalist, the type of Blue Labourist, cross-class coalition building, pro-worker, pro-business agenda outlined in this book – there is little hope of renewal across the party more broadly. Paul Keating is right: "Where goes NSW, so goes federal Labor." Of course, the former Labor prime minister wasn't just talking about the ALP's NSW branch, but his own right-wing Centre Unity faction, for better and now for the worse. The National Right lacks a coherent story about 'what it stands for' and tends to resist rather than initiate reform. For the Right, the '1983 and all that' school, the Hawke-Keating reform era fetish, is blocking the path to philosophical and policy renewal. There is no one on the horizon prepared to crash through and bang together the heads of the maddening array of sub-factions tearing the Right asunder.

The faction of earthy realism, in touch with the humble concerns of mainstream Australia, now veers between extremes – a Keating-style vanguardism that scorns public opinion, and a poll-driven fear of doing anything much at all. While many talented men and women fill its parliamentary and head office ranks, there is little sign of the intellectual and organisational renewal required to regain its potency. It continues to lose the battle of ideas within party ranks and, with those losses, controls fewer numbers. Too many young Laborites, if they do join the Right, struggle to identify a compelling ideological reason for joining in the first place. More than numbers, the Right has suffered from a perception of moral decline. In NSW the Graham Richardson creed of 'whatever it takes' has seemingly come to mean 'whatever we can take', as witnessed in the behaviour of the disgraced Health Services Union duo of Craig Thomson and Michael Williamson, and Joe Tripodi and Eddie Obeid, the former parliamentary duo who ruled the infamous NSW Right Terrigals' sub-faction in the NSW state parliament. Key figures, past and present, are in the pockets of Chinese Communist Party-aligned businesspeople and front organisations.

In 2011, in the wake of NSW Labor's implosion over electricity privatisation and subsequent electoral wipeout, Paul Keating eviscerated the machine-men of the faction he co-founded more than three decades earlier. "I think the problem with Centre Unity in NSW is that it lacks now an ideology ... other than the sheer pursuit of power ... But power for what?" History shows that the party is unlikely to renew its purpose without the Right's imprimatur. Although it acquired a reputation for anti-intellectualism, throughout the twentieth century the

Right was the driving force behind the party's central organising principle of labourism. In the 1980s, the Right buttressed the Hawke–Keating government's embrace of Labor's new big idea: a historic rebalancing of state and market forces that emptied out much of the labourist model. In 1993, the NSW Right's introduction of enterprise bargaining heralded a major shift away from centralised wage-fixing. It bequeathed Australia three decades of economic growth, but fatally weakened the Labor Right's raison d'être and in the latter case has led directly to our record low wages growth. The faction's renewal will demand its constituent parts adopt the broadest possible conception of acting from self-interest. The Right's renewal will demand courage, collectively and individually. Aristotle once defined courage as the middle way between recklessness and cowardice. For Labor's sake, and that of working people, the Right will need to pluck up a sufficient amount of that cardinal virtue to change its ways.

CONCLUSION

As we have seen throughout this book, the struggles of Australian Labor mirror those of its social democratic counterparts internationally. Adrian Pabst, drawing on Antonio Gramsci's idea of 'interregnum', traces this crisis through the arc of the post-World War Two world. "The centre-left is struggling to define itself at a time when the two models that have been dominant since 1945 are in crisis. First of all, the post-war settlement of 'embedded liberalism' that was regulated by Keynesian economics of full employment and underpinned by universal welfare. Secondly, the post-1970s settlement of 'neo-liberalism' that was driven by Hayekian economics of controlling inflation and enacting supply-side reforms. Social democracy built the first and embraced the second, but since the 2008-09 GFC nothing has replaced them."[221]

And so here we are. Yet to borrow a Howardism, the times can still suit Australian Labor. The national zeitgeist favours an activist, smart, big-hearted social democratic government focussed on tackling economic insecurity. It is hungry for long-term solutions on climate change and energy policy, housing affordability, healthcare and an ageing population, education from preschool to post-tertiary qualifications, the many manifestations of infrastructure and foreign policy, in short facing up to the challenge of dealing with both the threats and opportunities of our world. It expects a government to keep its word, to repair something of the frayed trust in our democratic institutions. Labor has before it a historic opportunity to shape a new long-term policy settlement, to build a modern, innovative, diversified, and egalitarian economy in a globalised world, and prepare us financially, and equip the nation institutionally, for decades to come. A settlement which will outlast a three-year term or political cycle, just as the Alfred Deakin-Labor alliance did in the federation decade, Curtin and Chifley managed after World War Two, and Hawke and Keating achieved in the 1980s and early 90s. The opportunity to redraw the lines of our settlement presents to very few generations. The nation-building settlements of the 1900s, 1940s and 1980s were spaced forty years apart and responded to seismic events a decade earlier. In an environment still shaped by the GFC, globalisation, technological disruption, inequality and democratic deficit, the time for a new settlement is now. The work must begin now and be put into practice by the next Labor government.

In 2013, delivering the George Lansbury memorial lecture, the British Labour MP Jon Cruddas wrote a call to arms to his own party. It is worth quoting at length. The task, as he saw it, "is about re-imagining what a Labour Party could be. This re-imagined socialism is romantic, not scientific; humane and warm; passionate yet humble; it is about rediscovering a political sentiment. It pushes back against party orthodoxy, careerism and transactional politics."[222] These words could have been uttered about the Australian Labor Party as it fell in 1996 and 2013. They ring even truer in 2019.

***

This book has been a labour of love, literally so. I write not out of anger, though I am angry at what transpired at the 2019 election and its lead-up, but out of admiration for a party which I have served, worked for, written about, torn my hair out over, celebrated, but above all loved. It remains the last, best hope for social democracy in this country. Love this book or hate it, my abiding hope is that readers do not feel indifference. The same is true of Labor. There will always be a minority of Australians who express antipathy towards the ALP. That is to be expected. It's what has bound together the parties of anti-Labor over more than a century. The real risk for Labor is the growing number of Australians who are joining their ranks and worse: working men and women and their families who mostly feel *indifferent* towards Labor. No political party has an innate right to exist. There is no guarantee Labor will be around in a few decades time, except as a historical footnote. It is possible to imagine this scenario and its awful consequences, as historian and Labor activist Janet McCalman eloquently describes: "Labor is an old party. That gives us deep values, loyal supporters, and long experience to draw on. But as we watch the fate of other old parties of the left and centre-left around the world, we must not take our past and our base for granted. If we allow Labor to wither, there is nothing to protect our people – working people, people without capital, people without homes, people without robust health, people without families to care for them, and people without regular work to fund their lives."[223] That thought should leave Laborites feeling really blue, but drive them – MPs, officials, members and affiliated unionists – to renew the party. The needs and aims driving working people to found Labor in 1891 remain relevant, and whether injected with ideas old, new, borrowed, and most definitely blue, they must be Labor's future too.

NOTES

Introduction

1   Elements of this section first appeared in Nick Dyrenfurth, 'Labor must stop blaming voters and start actually listening to them', *Australian Financial Review*, 22 May 2019, https://www.afr.com/politics/federal/labor-must-stop-blaming-voters-and-start-actually-listening-to-them-20190522-p51pxo

2   Frank Field, 'A Blue Labour Vision of the Common Good', in Ian Geary and Adrian Pabst (eds), *Blue Labour: Forging a New Politics*, IB Tauris, London, 2015, p. 60.

3   Nick Dyrenfurth, 'It's the Culture, Stupid!' in Nick Dyrenfurth and Tim Southphommasane (eds), *All That's Left: What Labor Should Stand For*, UNSW press, Sydney, 2010, pp. 15-36.

4   Geoff Gallop, 'How Labor Can Win in 2007', Unpublished paper, January 2007.

5   Paul Kelly, 'Beaten Labor commits to three more years in denial', *The Australian*, 25 May 2019, https://www.theaustralian.com.au/inquirer/beaten-labor-commits-to-three-more-years-in-denial/news-story/44a446e9a406776 59765b5245be691ea

Chapter One

6   Nick Bryant, 'Australia: Coup capital of the democratic world', *BBC News*, 14 September 2015, https://www.bbc.com/news/world-australia-34249214

7   Andrew Scott, *Fading Loyalties: The Australian Labor Party and the working class*, Pluto Press, Sydney, 1991, pp. 29-30; Norman Abjoronsen, 'The parties' democratic deficit', *Inside Story*, 10 February 2010, 'http://insidestory.org.au/the-parties-democratic-deficit/

8   Liberal Party of Australia, 'Our Structure', https://www.liberal.org.au/our-structure

9   Troy Bramston, 'Members flee Labor despite Shorten's target', *The Australian*, 17 April 2018, https://www.theaustralian.com.au/nation/politics/members-flee-labor-despite-shortens-target/news-story/b1da2d450780aa14eac5ecbff2dd7360

10 See, generally, Judith Brett, *Australian Liberals and the Moral Middle Class: From Alfred Deakin to John Howard*, Cambridge University Press, 2003.

11 Shane Granger, 'QuikStats: Australian Political Party Membership', *Randon Analytica*, 15 October 2013, https://randomanalytica.com/2013/10/15/quikstats-australian-political-party-membership/

12 George Megalogenis, 'Australia Divided', *The Monthly*, December 2016, https://www.themonthly.com.au/issue/2016/december/1480510800/george-megalogenis/australia-divided

13 Peter Khalil, 'Workers of the World', *The Tocsin*, no. 1, June 2017, pp. 12-14.

14 Abigail Lewis, 'The Way In: Representation in the Australian Parliament', January 2019, *Per Capita*, https://percapita.org.au/wp-content/uploads/2019/01/The-Way-In-Representation-in-the-Australian-Parliament-2.pdf

15 John Hirst, *Sense and Nonsense in Australian History*, Black Inc., Melbourne, 2009, p. 172.

16 Emma Dawson, 'We're not all postmaterialists now', *The Tocsin*, no. 7, July 2019, p. 9.

17 Urban Sila and Valéry Dugain, 'Income, wealth and earnings inequality in Australia: Evidence from the HILDA survey', Economics Department Working Papers, No. 1538, Organisation for Economic Co-operation and Development, 14 February 2019, http://www.oecd.org/officialdocuments/publicdisplaydocumentpdf/?cote=ECO/WKP(2019)7&docLanguage=En

18 Shane Wright and Eryk Bagshaw, 'Revealed: The households with surging wealth and the households standing still', *Sydney Morning Herald*, 12 July 2019, https://www.smh.com.au/politics/federal/revealed-the-households-with-surging-wealth-and-the-households-standing-still-20190712-p526js.html

19 OECD, 'Under Pressure: The Squeezed Middle Class', Organisation for Economic Co-operation and Development, 1 May 2019, https://www.oecd.org/social/under-pressure-the-squeezed-middle-class-689afed1-en.htm

20 Nick Dyrenfurth, *Make Australia Fair Again: the Case for Employee Representatives on Company Boards*, John Curtin Research Centre, Melbourne, 2017, pp. 10-11.

21 Nick Dyrenfurth, 'The case for a living wage has never been stronger', *The Age*, 14 March 2019, https://www.theage.com.au/national/the-case-for-a-living-wage-has-never-been-stronger-20190314-p5145i.html

22 David Uren, 'Low-paid workers and wage theft', *The Saturday Paper*, 3 August 2019, https://www.thesaturdaypaper.com.au/news/politics/2019/08/03/low-paid-workers-and-wage-theft/15647544008552

23 Australian Council of Social Service, 'Poverty in Australia', *ACOSS*, 16 October 2018, https://www.acoss.org.au/wp-content/uploads/2018/10/ACOSS_Poverty-in-Australia-Report_Web-Final.pdf

24 Nick Dyrenfurth, *Super Ideas: Securing Australia's Retirement Income System*, John Curtin Research Centre in conjunction with Vision Super, Melbourne, 2018.

25 Dyrenfurth, *Make Australia Fair Again*, p. 10.

26 Nick Dyrenfurth, *#Changethestats: a new way of talking about unemployment*, John Curtin Research Centre, Melbourne, 2019, https://www.curtinrc.org/changethestats

27 Greg Jericho, 'No matter your age or gender - there is no escaping the underemployment boom', *Guardian Australia*, 23 October 2018, https://www.theguardian.com/business/grogonomics/2018/oct/22/no-matter-your-age-or-gender-there-is-no-escaping-the-underemployment-boom

28 Dyrenfurth, *#Changethestats*.

29 'Australia's future workforce?', Committee for Economic Development of Australia, https://www.ceda.com.au/Research-and-policy/All-CEDA-research/Research-catalogue/Australia-s-future-workforce

30 Wayne Swan, 'Restoring class balance: bargaining power and full employment in the 21st century', Speech to the 2017 ACTU Congress, Sydney, 26 June 2017, https://swanmp.org/news-media/speeches/speech-restoring-class-

balance-bargaining-power-and-full-employment-in-the-21st-century/

31 Florence Jaumotte and Carolina Osorio, 'Inequality and Labor Market Institutions', IMF Staff Discussion Note, July 2015, https://www.imf.org/external/pubs/ft/sdn/2015/sdn1514.pdf, p. 27.

32 Gray Connolly, 'Conservative Futures', *Meanjin*, Autumn 2016, https://meanjin.com.au/essays/conservative-futures/; https://twitter.com/GrayConnolly/status/970383181420494848

33 Essential Vision, 'Essential Report: Change for Classes', 29 November 2016, http://www.essentialvision.com.au/change-for-classes

34 'Community pulse 2018: the economic disconnect', Committee for Economic Development of Australia, https://www.ceda.com.au/Research-and-policy/All-CEDA-research/Research-catalogue/Community-pulse-2018-the-economic-disconnect

35 Shane Wright and Eryk Bagshaw, 'Australian economy slows to lowest rate in five years', *Sydney Morning Herald*, 5 June 2019, https://www.smh.com.au/business/the-economy/economy-slows-to-lowest-rate-in-five-years-20190605-p51un8.html

36 Dyrenfurth, *Make Australia Fair Again.*

37 Shane Wright, 'The two charts showing an extraordinary collapse in home ownership in Sydney and Melbourne', *Sydney Morning Herald*, 17 July 2019, https://www.smh.com.au/politics/federal/the-two-charts-showing-an-extraordinary-collapse-in-home-ownership-in-sydney-and-melbourne-20190717-p5282j.html

38 Greg Jericho, 'Interest rates are lower than ever. So why is owning a home harder than ever?', *Guardian Australia*, 5 June 2018, https://www.theguardian.com/business/grogonomics/2018/jun/05/interest-rates-are-lower-than-ever-so-why-is-owning-a-home-harder-than-ever

39 David Taylor, "We've never seen it as bad as it is': Researchers warn of rising mortgage stress', *ABC News*, 5 April 2019, https://www.abc.net.au/news/2019-04-05/researchers-warn-of-rising-mortgage-stress/10972682

40 'Census 2016: More Aussies now renting, but paying extra', *Rent.com.au*, https://www.rent.com.au/blog/renting-rise-census-2016

41 Productivity Commission, 'Report on Government Services 2019', https://www.pc.gov.au/research/ongoing/report-on-government-services/2019/housing-and-homelessness

42 Adrian Pabst, 'Politics of the void: how the left abandoned patriotism and the common good', *New Statesman*, 22 August 2018, https://www.newstatesman.com/politics/uk/2018/08/politics-void-how-left-abandoned-patriotism-and-common-good

43 Kim Carr, 'The Task Ahead', *The Tocsin*, no. 7, July 2019, p. 5.

44 Tony Judt, *Ill Fares the Land: A Treatise On Our Present Discontents*, Penguin, London, 2011, 'Conclusion'.

45 https://twitter.com/hughriminton/status/1031725249795055617

46 Quoted in Jessica Irvine, 'The policy chaos eroding our faith in democracy', *Sydney Morning Herald*, 19 November 2018, https://www.smh.com.au/national/the-policy-chaos-eroding-our-faith-in-democracy-20181115-p50g8l.html

47 Patrick Weller and Sue Fraser, 'The younging of Australian politics or politics as first career', *Australian Journal of Political Science*, vol. 2, no. 2, 1987, pp. 76-83.

48 George Megalogenis 'Blowing up the government to save it', *The Monthly*, October 2018, https://www.themonthly.com.au/issue/2018/october/1538316000/george-megalogenis/blowing-government-save-it

49 Gareth Hutchens, 'Australians no longer trust their democracy, survey finds', *Guardian Australia*, 5 December 2018, https://www.theguardian.com/australia-news/2018/dec/05/australians-no-longer-trust-their-democracy-survey-finds

50 Alex Oliver, '2018 Lowy Institute Poll', 20 June 2018, https://www.lowyinstitute.org/publications/2018-lowy-institute-poll

51 Leader, 'Aussie Rules: What the world can learn from Australia', *The Economist*, 27 October 2018, https://www.economist.com/leaders/2018/10/27/what-the-world-can-learn-from-australia

Chapter Two

52 Jim Chalmers, 'Austalgia: Our Homesickness for the Past', *Meanjin*, vol. 74, no. 3, 2015, https://meanjin.com.au/essays/austalgia-our-homesickness-for-the-past/.

53 Jonathan Freedland, 'Personality Politics', *Guardian*, 3 March 2007, https://www.theguardian.com/commentisfree/2007/mar/02/isharesomeofjackie

54 Paul Strangio and James Walter, *No, Prime Minister: Reclaiming Politics from Leaders*, UNSW Press, Sydney, 2007.

55 Jessica Irvine, 'The policy chaos eroding our faith in democracy', *Sydney Morning Herald*, 19 November 2018, https://www.smh.com.au/national/the-policy-chaos-eroding-our-faith-in-democracy-20181115-p50g8l.html

56 John Harding-Easson, 'Farewell Freudy', Facebook post, 26 July 2019.

57 Paul Strangio, 'Has Labor's messiah complex finally taught it a tough lesson?', *The Age*, 27 February 2012, https://www.theage.com.au/politics/federal/has-labors-messiah-complex-finally-taught-it-a-tough-lesson-20120226-1twdo.html

58 Quoted from Geoff Gallop, 'Whitlam's hard fight for reform holds lessons for Labor today', *The Conversation*, 22 October 2014, https://theconversation.com/whitlams-hard-fight-for-reform-holds-lessons-for-labor-today-33264

59 Quoted from Ross McMullin, *The Light on the Hill: the Australian Labor Party, 1891–1991*, Oxford University Press, Melbourne, 1992, pp. 57–8.

60 Quoted from Nick Dyrenfurth, *Heroes and Villains: the Rise and Fall of the Early Australian Labor Party*, Australian Scholarly Publishing, Melbourne, 2011, p. 185.

61 ibid, p. 219.

62 Megalogenis 'Blowing up the government to save it'.

63 Bill Shorten, 'Per Capita Forum', Melbourne, 25 September 2013, https://www.billshorten.com.au/per-capita-forum-wheeler-centre-melbourne

64 This section draws on Nick Dyrenfurth, 'Back to the Future: 1983 and all that', *The Age*, 28 December 2013, http://www.theage.com.au/national/back-to-the-future-1983-and-all-that-20131227-2zzhl.html

65   Chalmers, 'Austalgia'.

66   Deborah Snow, 'Paul Keating says neo-liberalism is at 'a dead end' after Sally McManus speech', *Sydney Morning Herald*, 30 March 2017, https://www.smh.com.au/politics/federal/paul-keating-says-neoliberalism-is-at-a-dead-end-after-sally-mcmanus-speech-20170329-gv9cto.html

67   Quotes from Nick Dyrenfurth, 'A man for some seasons', *The Monthly*, 23 September 2015, https://www.themonthly.com.au/blog/nick-dyrenfurth/2015/23/2015/1442978238/man-some-seasons

68   This sections draws on Dyrenfurth, 'A man for some seasons' and Nick Dyrenfurth, 'In search of Turnbull's mojo', *The Monthly*, 20 October 2016, https://www.themonthly.com.au/blog/nick-dyrenfurth/2016/20/2016/1476939654/search-turnbull-s-mojo

69   Quoted from Graham Richardson, *Whatever it Takes*, Bantam Books, Sydney, 1994, pp. 46–47.

70   These sections draw on Nick Dyrenfurth, 'Howard's chickens come home to roost', *The Monthly*, 21 April 2017, https://www.themonthly.com.au/blog/nick-dyrenfurth/2017/21/2017/1492754557/howard-s-chickens-come-home-roost, and Nick Dyrenfurth, 'Howard's children', *The Monthly*, 13 April 2017, https://www.themonthly.com.au/blog/nick-dyrenfurth/2017/13/2017/1492059253/howard-s-children

71   Emily Millane, 'Tinkering can achieve a lot: politics isn't broken', *The Conversation*, 5 November 2018, https://theconversation.com/tinkering-can-achieve-a-lot-politics-isnt-broken-105819

72   David Crowe, *Venom: the Vendettas and Betrayals That Broke a Party*, HarperCollins, Sydney, 2019, p.337.

Chapter Three

73   Bill Shorten, 'Maiden speech to parliament', 14 February 2008. https://australianpolitics.com/2008/02/14/bill-shorten-maiden-speech.html

74   Bill Shorten, 'The New Centre', *Arena Magazine* in conjunction with the Australian Fabian Society, December 2004, no. 74, pp. 9-10.

75   Quoted in Katharine Murphy, 'Labor must be more than "Bob and Paul's dumb-arse stepkids"', *Guardian Australia*, 28 September 2014, https://www.theguardian.com/world/2014/sep/28/labor-must-be-more-than-bob-and-pauls-dumb-arse-step-kids

76   Geoff Robinson, 'Review: Faction Man – Bill Shorten's Path to Power', *The Conversation*, 12 October 2015, https://theconversation.com/review-faction-man-bill-shortens-path-to-power-47752

77   Neal Blewett, 'The assassination of Rudd', *Australian Book Review*, September 2010, p. 10.

78   Jenny Hocking, *A Moment in History: Gough Whitlam: The Biography, Volume 1*, Melbourne University Publishing, Melbourne, p. 279.

79   Frank Bongiorno, 'Why Bill Shorten is not a socialist', *The Conversation*, 7 March 2018, https://theconversation.com/mis-red-why-bill-shorten-is-not-a-socialist-91752

80   Paul Strangio, 'Shorten the consensus leader unites a fractured Labor, but it may

not quite be enough', *The Conversation*, 20 June 2016, https://theconversation. com/shorten-the-consensus-leader-unites-a-fractured-labor-but-it-may-not-quite-be-enough-61741

81   Nick Dyrenfurth, 'Labor's British Blues', *The Monthly*, 19 May 2015, http:// www.themonthly.com.au/blog/nick-dyrenfurth/2015/19/2015/1432004548/ labor-s-british-blues

Chapter Four

82   Scott Morrison, 'Press Conference – Thursday 11 April 2019', https://www. liberal.org.au/latest-news/2019/04/11/press-conference-thursday-11-april-2019

83   Don Watson, *Recollections of a Bleeding Heart: A portrait of Paul Keating PM*, Knopf, Sydney, 2002, p. 732.

84   Bill Shorten, 'Doorstop – Mitcham – Thursday 11 April', https://www. billshorten.com.au/doorstop_mitcham_thursday_11_april_2019

85   Amy Remeikis, '"Shorten wants to end the weekend": Morrison attacks Labor's electric vehicle policy', *Guardian Australia*, 7 April 2019, https://www. theguardian.com/australia-news/2019/apr/07/shorten-wants-to-end-the-weekend-morrison-attacks-labors-electric-vehicle-policy

86   Frank Bongiorno, 'As election 2019 kicks off, the only certainty is a cranky and mistrustful electorate', *The Conversation*, 11 April 2019, https:// theconversation.com/as-election-2019-kicks-off-the-only-certainty-is-a-cranky-and-mistrustful-electorate-113659

87   Katharine Murphy and Paul Karp, 'Labor fumes at "dodgy Treasury costings" as Coalition alleges "tax hit on the economy"', *Guardian Australia*, 11 April 2019, https://www.theguardian.com/australia-news/2019/apr/11/labor-fumes-at-dodgy-treasury-costings-as-coalition-alleges-tax-hit-on-the-economy

88   Joe Kelly, 'Property agents unite to fight negative gearing crackdown', *The Australian*, 12 April 2019, https://www.theaustralian.com.au/nation/politics/ property-agents-unite-to-fight-negative-gearing-crackdown/news-story/ c13d61201df6e06973f7dad16147f188

89   Essential Research, 'The Essential Report: 6 May 2019', https://www. essentialvision.com.au/wp-content/uploads/2019/05/Essential-Report-060519.pdf

90   Dennis Shanahan, 'Polling goes Coalition's way, Newspoll data shows', *The Australian*, 16 April 2019, https://www.theaustralian.com.au/nation/ politics/voters-who-once-turned-on-turnbull-are-flocking-back/news-story/ aaa9cccd033099fef632a820cf393cf5

91   John Kehoe and Phillip Coorey, 'Morrison tax plan needs $40b spending cut', *Australian Financial Review*, 16 April 2019, https://www.afr.com/politics/ federal/morrison-s-plan-requires-40b-cut-20190415-p51e6l

92   Paddy Manning, 'Greens bid for relevance', *The Monthly*, 1 May 2019, https:// www.themonthly.com.au/today/paddy-manning/2019/01/2019/1556689673/ greens-bid-relevance

93   Malcolm Farr, 'Bill Shorten's blind spot exposed on the campaign trail', *News. com.au*, 18 April 2019, https://www.news.com.au/national/federal-election/ bill-shortens-blind-spot-exposed-on-the-campaign-trail/news-story/ ef5670dd8f41b514cbd82b7d39d3a55e

94   Phillip Coorey, 'Labor suddenly looks exposed', *Australian Financial Review*, 17 April 2019, https://www.afr.com/politics/federal/labor-suddenly-looks-exposed-20190416-p51et8

95   Troy Bramston, 'Verdict: Who won the Week', *The Australian*, 19 April 2019,https://www.theaustralian.com.au/commentary/federal-election-2019-our-verdict-on-week-one-of-the-campaign/news-story/f1b79880b-178261f9e3894cb33d66749

96   Theo Theophanous, 'Campaigns are brutal but Bill Shorten has to tough it out', *Herald Sun*, 23 April 2019, https://www.heraldsun.com.au/news/opinion/theo-theophanous-campaigns-are-brutal-but-bill-shorten-has-to-tough-it-out/news-story/ea02ad09945f5edcd0c2df5c2ffcfba6

97   Joe Kelly, 'Shorten was being polite to worker', *The Australian*, 24 April 2019, https://www.theaustralian.com.au/nation/shorten-was-being-polite-to-worker/news-story/32263cfb128c3e19b1e54e548fa8095b

98   Samantha Maiden, 'Bill Shorten edges PM in first leaders debate', *The New Daily*, 30 April 2019, https://thenewdaily.com.au/news/election-2019/2019/04/30/morrison-shorten-debate/

99   Simon Benson, 'Newspoll: Bill Shorten's billion-dollar promises fail to prevent slide in popularity', *The Australian*, 6 May 2019, https://www.theaustralian.com.au/nation/politics/newspoll-promises-fail-to-prevent-bill-shortens-slide-in-popularity/news-story/51ca4e3f1405aaa275022e0e2a2b6ef0

100 AAP, 'Clive Palmer: Sacked Queensland Nickel worker payouts not my burden', *Sydney Morning Herald*, https://www.smh.com.au/business/companies/clive-palmer-sacked-queensland-nickel-worker-payouts-not-my-burden-20160126-gme28b.html

101 Peter Brent, 'It's not what you ask, it's how you ask it', *Inside Story*, 27 April 2019, https://insidestory.org.au/its-not-what-you-ask-its-how-you-ask-it/

102 Michelle Grattan, 'View from The Hill: Bill Shorten at ease in town hall-type forum', *The Conversation*, 3 May 2019, https://theconversation.com/view-from-the-hill-bill-shorten-at-ease-in-town-hall-type-forum-116555

103 Katharine Murphy, 'Former PMs bury the hatchet in show of unity at Labor campaign launch', *Guardian Australia*, 5 May 2019, https://www.theguardian.com/australia-news/2019/may/05/former-pms-bury-the-hatchet-in-show-of-unity-at-labor-campaign-launch

104 Dennis Shanahan, 'Local issues and a patchwork quilt of seats will be decisive', *The Australian*, 5 May 2019, https://www.theaustralian.com.au/nation/politics/a-patchwork-quilt-of-seats-will-be-decisive/news-story/a9ecc97fc63c057e91758bd0d603fb3d

105 Tony Wright, 'Vintage Paul Keating steals the best lines at Bill Shorten's big show', *Sydney Morning Herald*, 5 May 2019, https://www.smh.com.au/federal-election-2019/vintage-paul-keating-steals-the-best-lines-at-bill-shorten-s-big-show-20190505-p51kab.html

106 Amy Remeikis, 'Shorten condemns egging of Australian prime minister Scott Morrison – as it happened', *Guardian Australia*, 7 May 2019, https://www.theguardian.com/australia-news/live/2019/may/07/federal-election-2019-shorten-morrison-coalition-labor-poll-politics-live?page=with:-block-5cd0f9a88f084f582f89478a

107 Anna Caldwell, 'Labor leader Bill Shorten's heartfelt story about his mother was missing one vital fact', *Daily Telegraph*, 8 May 2019, https://www.dailytelegraph.com.au/news/nsw/labor-leader-bill-shortens-heartfelt-story-about-his-mother-was-missing-one-vital-fact/news-story/eeab8c4d16e-3f55304e06eaa704699c9

108 David Crowe, 'Bill Shorten close to tears as he condemns newspaper over story about his mother', *Sydney Morning Herald*, 8 May 2019, https://www.smh.com.au/federal-election-2019/bill-shorten-attacks-newspaper-over-story-about-his-mother-20190508-p51l48.html

109 Andrew Bolt, 'I understand Shorten's anger', *Herald Sun*, 8 May 2019, https://www.heraldsun.com.au/blogs/andrew-bolt/i-understand-shortens-anger/news-story/83c6431ee6562d7a155707c8384ec3ff

110 Nick Dyrenfurth, 'The Daily Telegraph's slipshod hit on Bill Shorten', *The Monthly*, 9 May 2019, https://www.themonthly.com.au/blog/nick-dyrenfurth/2019/09/2019/1557366571/daily-telegraph-s-slipshod-hit-bill-shorten

111 Sarah Martin, 'Campaign catchup 2019: Shorten hits back at News Corp in mother of all rows', *Guardian Australia*, 8 May 2019, https://www.theguardian.com/australia-news/2019/may/08/campaign-catchup-2019-shorten-attacks-news-corp-in-mother-of-all-rows

112 Quoted from David Marr, 'Faction Man: Bill Shorten's Pursuit of Power', *Quarterly Essay* 59, 2015, p. 17.

113 Paul Kelly, 'Numbers demonstrate a turning point: Shorten's ready to govern', *The Australian*, 11 May 2019, https://www.theaustralian.com.au/commentary/numbers-demonstrate-a-turning-point-shortens-ready-to-govern/news-story/51c1c53d0378daob8cf6fe24ec85fc76

114 AAP, 'Newspoll shows Labor still just ahead, with boost to Bill Shorten's personal rating', *Guardian Australia*, 13 May 2019, https://www.theguardian.com/australia-news/2019/may/13/newspoll-shows-labor-still-just-ahead-with-boost-to-bill-shortens-personal-rating

115 Shannon Molloy, 'Federal election 2019: Kerri-Anne Kennerley's huge call — Bill Shorten will 'end life as we know it', *News.com.au*, 15 May 2019, https://www.news.com.au/entertainment/tv/morning-shows/federal-election-2019-kerrianne-kennerleys-huge-call-bill-shorten-will-end-life-as-we-know-it/news-story/86508c8610f70bdad6b596b179b76ac7

116 Adrian Pabst, *The Story of Our Country: Labor's vision for Australia*, Kapunda Press (Connor Court), Brisbane, 2019, p. 24.

Chapter Five

117 Paul Rodan, 'Labor's numbers game', *Inside Story*, 30 May 2019, https://insidestory.org.au/labors-numbers-game/?fbclid=IwARoZpjeKFHWt-m81AE-oBufEZF4W1bOldZmsYLd3ZYt6inSLpxRlkMjBYc68

118 Kosmos Samaras, 'Labor's Culture War', *The Tocsin*, no. 7, July 2019, p. 11.

119 This section draws on Nick Dyrenfurth, 'Australia', in Adrian Pabst and Neal Lawson (eds), *What's Left: The state of global social democracy and lessons for UK Labour*, University of Kent/Compass, United Kingdom, 2018.

120 Michael Easson, "Edmund Burke and Australian Labor", in Damien Freeman (ed.), *The Market's Morals: Responding to Jesse Norman*, Kapunda Press (Connor Court) Redland Bay, forthcoming 2019.

121 Pabst, *The Story of Our Country*, p. 189.

122 Peter Baldwin, 'A nation shows its true colours', *The Australian*, 25 May 2019, https://www.theaustralian.com.au/inquirer/black-swan-poll-result-helps-nation-show-its-true-colours/news-story/2c1ddcf2d6dc9aed6925445bef-17f2a6

123 Jonathan Rutherford, 'How the decline of the working class made Labour a party of the bourgeois left', *New Statesman*, 19 September 2018, https://www.newstatesman.com/politics/uk/2018/09/how-decline-working-class-made-labour-party-bourgeois-left?fbclid=IwAR0_RPVAnY-alEKl8X7T8S5kGC1ucoQ-zL1w3fcTSn3CrRIHoHpvmofilpu4

124 Sheri Berman, 'Why identity politics benefits the right more than the left', *Guardian*, 14 July 2019, https://www.theguardian.com/commentisfree/2018/jul/14/identity-politics-right-left-trump-racism

125 Maurice Glasman, 'The Good Society, Catholic Social Thought and the Politics of the Common Good', in Ian Geary and Adrian Pabst (eds), *Blue Labour: Forging a New Politics*, IB Tauris, London, 2015, p. 13 and more generally, Chapter One.

126 Jim Waterson, 'Labour Peer Maurice Glasman Says His Party Will Lose Because "It Doesn't Believe What The People Believe"', *Buzz Feed News*, 21 May 2017, https://www.buzzfeed.com/jimwaterson/labour-peer-maurice-glasman-says-his-party-will-lose

127 Elements of the following passages are drawn from Nick Dyrenfurth and Frank Bongiorno, *A Little History of the Australian Labor Party*, UNSW press, Sydney, 2011.

128 Albert Métin, *Socialism Without Doctrine*, trans. Russel Ward, Alternative Publishing Co-operative, Sydney, 1977.

129 Maurice Glasman, 'Britain can prosper by understanding how Germany succeeds', *New Statesman*, 1 May 2013, https://www.newstatesman.com/politics/uk-politics/2013/05/britain-can-prosper-understanding-how-germany-succeeds

130 The classic expression is Bede Nairn, *Civilising Capitalism: The Labor Movement in New South Wales 1870–1900*, Australian National University (ANU) Press, Canberra, 1973.

131 This section draws on Dyrenfurth, 'Back to the Future: 1983 and all that'.

132 James Frost, 'Which crisis of trust?', *Inside Story*, 18 July 2019, https://insidestory.org.au/which-crisis-of-trust/

133 Frank Bongiorno, 'Blue Labour: Lessons for Australia', Australian Fabians, 2012, http://www.fabians.org.au/blue_labour_lessons_for_australia

134 Troy Bramston (ed.), *The Whitlam Legacy*, Federation Press, Sydney, 2015.

135 Elements of this section draw on Nick Dyrenfurth, *A powerful influence on Australian affairs: a new history of the AWU*, Melbourne University Publishing, Carlton, 2017, Chapters 1-4.

136 Dyrenfurth, *Heroes and Villains*, Ch. 1.

137 Quoted in Dyrenfurth, *Heroes and Villains*, p. 58.

138 Ben Chifley, 'The Light on the Hill', Speech to the NSW Labor Party Conference, 12 June 1949, https://www.chifley.org.au/the-light-on-the-hill/

139 Rutherford, 'How the decline of the working class made Labour a party of the bourgeois left'.

140 Dyrenfurth, *Heroes and Villains*, Ch. 2; *Dyrenfurth and Bongiorno*, A Little History of the ALP, Ch. 1.

141 Roger Scruton, 'The failure to stand up for conservative thinking is leading us into a new cultural dark age', *The Telegraph* (London), 20 July 2019, https://www.telegraph.co.uk/politics/2019/07/20/failure-stand-conservative-thinking-leading-us-new-cultural/

142 William Guthrie Spence, *Australia's Awakening: Thirty Years in the Life of an Australian Agitator*, Worker Trustees, Sydney, 1909, cited at http://purl.library.usyd.edu.au/setis/id/fed0036

143 This section draws on Nick Dyrenfurth, 'William Guthrie Spence: "Father" of the Australian Workers Union', in W. G. Spence, *History of the AWU*, Melbourne University Press, Melbourne, (2013 [1911]).

144 *The Worker* (Sydney), 4 June 1892, p. 1.

145 William Guthrie Spence, *Lesson of History*, Worker Print, Sydney, 1908, p. 16.

146 Andrew Leigh, 'Social liberalism fits Labor', *The Saturday Paper*, 29 June 2019, https://www.thesaturdaypaper.com.au/opinion/topic/2019/06/29/social-liberalism-fits-labor/15617304008366

147 Chris Bowen, *Hearts & Minds*: A Blueprint for Modern Labor, Melbourne University Publishing, Melbourne, 2013.

148 Nick Evershed, 'The eight charts that help explain why the Coalition won the 2019 Australian election', *Guardian Australia*, 22 May 2019, https://www.theguardian.com/news/datablog/2019/may/22/the-eight-charts-that-help-explain-why-the-coalition-won-the-2019-australian-election?

149 Mike Seccombe, 'How seniors became our most fierce lobby', *The Saturday Paper*, 20 July 2019, https://www.thesaturdaypaper.com.au/news/politics/2019/07/20/how-seniors-became-our-most-fierce-lobby/15635448008454

150 Paul Collier, 'Denmark has shown how to renew European social democracy', *New Statesman*, 10 June 2019, https://www.newstatesman.com/world/europe/2019/06/denmark-has-shown-how-renew-european-social-democracy

151 Quoted from Nick Dyrenfurth, 'Liberalism is alive and it is killing us: why postliberalism is the answer', *The Age*, 7 September 2014, http://www.theage.com.au/federal-politics/political-opinion/liberalism-is-alive-and-its-killing-us-why-postliberalism-is-the-answer-20140903-108v50.html

152 Maurice Glasman, 'Labour as a Radical Tradition', in Maurice Glasman, Jonathan Rutherford, *Marc Stears* and Stuart White (eds) *The Labour Tradition and the Politics of Paradox: The Oxford London Seminars 2010-11*, Oxford London Seminars in association with the Christian Socialist Movement, Compass, the Fabian Society, Progress and *Soundings Journal*, June 2011, https://www.lwbooks.co.uk/book/labour-tradition-and-politics-paradox.

153 Quoted in Nick Cater, 'UK Labour luminary Maurice Glasman unimpressed

by ALP's efforts', *The Australian*, 3 August 2013. ttps://www.theaustralian.com.au/opinion/columnists/uk-labour-luminary-maurice-glasman-unimpressed-by-alps-efforts/news-story/e2f3cee74a6d461bbae1ff7f9b95ad63

154   Maurice Glasman, 'One Nation: Reconciling the plurality and diversity of existing interests and traditions in pursuit of the common good', *London School of Economics*, 29 May 2013, http://blogs.lse.ac.uk/politicsandpolicy/one-nation-tradition-virtue-and-modernity/

155   Bongiorno, 'Blue Labour'.

156   This section draws on Dyrenfurth, 'Liberalism is alive and it is killing us'.

157   Philip Blond, *Red Tory: How Left and Right Have Broken Britain and How We Can Fix It*, Faber, London, 2010.

158   David Goodhart, *A Postliberal Future?*, Demos, London, 2014, https://www.demos.co.uk/files/apostliberalfuture.pdf

159   ibid

160   Dennis Glover, *An Economy Is Not A Society*, Redback, Melbourne, 2015.

161   Kosmos Samaras, 'The Return of the Working Class', *The Tocsin*, June 2017, p. 10.

162   J.D. Vance, *Hillbilly Elegy: A Memoir of a Family and Culture in Crisis*, HarperCollins, London, p. 1.

163   Jennifer Rayner, 'The blue-collar decline', *The Tocsin*, no.3, December 2017, p. 16. See, in greater depth, Jennifer Rayner, *Blue Collar Frayed: What's Not Working for Australian Men*, Black Inc, Melbourne, 2018.

164   Goodhart, *A Postliberal Future?*

Chapter Six

165   Quoted in Graham Freudenberg, 'Victory to Defeat: 1941–49', in John Faulkner and Stuart Macintyre (eds), T*rue Believers: The story of the Federal Parliamentary Labor Party*, Allen & Unwin, Sydney, 2001, p. 79.

166   Forestry and Furnishing Products Division of the Construction, Forestry, Mining and Energy Union, 'The Brompton Report: A new approach for Labor', http://www.onlineopinion.com.au/documents/articles/brompton_report.pdf

167   Quoted from Nick Dyrenfurth, 'Back to the people', *The Monthly*, 27 November 2015, https://www.themonthly.com.au/blog/nick-dyrenfurth/2015/27/2015/1448582891/back-people.

168   Robin Archer, *Why Is There No Labor Party in the United States?*, Princeton University Press, Princeton, 2007, p. 1.

169   This section draws on Dyrenfurth, 'Australia'.

170   Jonathan Rutherford, 'How the decline of the working class made Labour a party of the bourgeois left', *New Statesman*, 19 September 2018, https://www.newstatesman.com/politics/uk/2018/09/how-decline-working-class-made-labour-party-bourgeois-left

171   Michael Thompson, *Labor's Forgotten People: The Triumph of Identity Politics*, Connor Court, Brisbane, 2019, p. 16.

172   Tim Gattrell, 'Could Chifley win preselection today?', Address to the NSW

Fabian Society, 20 April 2005, https://www.fabians.org.au/could_chifley_ win_preselection_today_gartrell

173 This section draws on Nick Dyrenfurth, 'Why rev-head Ricky Muir is really a Labor man', *The Monthly*, 6 March 2015, https://www.themonthly.com.au/ blog/nick-dyrenfurth/2015/06/2015/1425610842/why-rev-head-ricky-muir- really-labor-man

174 I draw here on Nick Dyrenfurth, 'It's time Labor went back to the workers', *The Weekend Australian*, 22 October 2011, http://www.theaustralian.com. au/national-affairs/opinion/its-time-labor-went-back-to-the-workers/sto- ry-e6frgdox-1226173497722

175 Luke Walladge, 'Stephen Conroy: the last of the Mohicans', *Spectator Aus- tralia*, 16 September 2016, https://www.spectator.com.au/2016/09/ste- phen-conroy-the-last-of-the-mohicans/?fbclid=IwAR211CydkD7kAkuuFl- 9R2W5flnqW7Vtkw9ChwqDaQHRFeBR3QUqxcIw3JHo

176 Kosmos Samaras, 'Labor's Culture War', *The Tocsin*, no. 7, July 2019, p. 11.

177 This section draws on Dyrenfurth, 'Australia'.

178 Carr, 'The Task Ahead', p. 5.

179 Olaf Cramme, Patrick Diamond and Michael McTernan, *A Centre-Left Proj- ect for New Times*, Policy Network, London, 2012.

180 This section draws on Nick Dyrenfurth, *Make Australia Fair Again: the Case for Employee Representatives on Company Boards*, John Curtin Research Centre, Melbourne, 2017.

181 Steven Hill, *Europe's Promise: Why the European Way is the Best Hope in an Insecure Age*, University of California Press, United States, 2010, p. 55.

182 Sigurt Vitols, *Prospects for trade unions in the evolving European system of corporate governance*, European Trade Union Institute for Research, Education and Health and Safety, Brussels, 2005, http://library.fes.de/pdf- files/gurn/00299.pdf

183 The Gini index measures the distribution of income across income percen- tiles in a population. A higher Gini index indicates greater inequality, with high income individuals receiving much larger percentages of the total in- come of the population and vice versa.

184 Felix Hörisch, 'The Macro-Economic Effect of Codetermination on Income Equality', Mannheimer Zentrum für Europäische Sozialforschung, no. 147, December 2012, https://papers.ssrn.com/sol3/papers.cfm?abstract_ id=2187264

185 Industry 4.0 can be understood as the current point of rapid technological change that is fundamentally changing how businesses conduct their opera- tions across all industries.

186 Nick O'Malley, 'How Germany closed its coal industry without sacking a sin- gle miner', *Sydney Morning Herald*, 14 July 2019, https://www.smh.com.au/ environment/climate-change/how-germany-closed-its-coal-industry-with- out-sacking-a-single-miner-20190711-p526ez.html

187 Briefing, 'The good and bad in Germany's economic model are strongly linked', *The Economist*, 8 July 2017, https://www.economist.com/news/brief- ing/21724801-germany-admired-its-stability-derided-persistent-trade-sur- pluses-good-and-bad

188 Jonathan Michie, 'How Britain could benefit by bringing workers into the boardroom', *The Conversation*, 12 October 2016, https://theconversation.com/how-britain-could-benefit-by-bringing-workers-into-the-boardroom-66693

189 Larry Elliot, 'The UK could learn a lot from Germany's long-term industrial strategy', *Guardian*, 31 March 2016, https://www.theguardian.com/global/2016/mar/30/the-uk-could-learn-a-lot-from-germanys-long-term-industrial-strategy

190 Trading Economics, 'Australia - Manufacturing, value added (% of GDP)', https://tradingeconomics.com/australia/manufacturing-value-added-percent-of-gdp-wb-data.html

191 Elliot, 'The UK could learn a lot from Germany's long-term industrial strategy'.

192 High Pay Centre, 'Workers on boards: interviews with German employee directors', 16 September 2013, http://highpaycentre.org/pubs/workers-on-boards-interviews-with-German-employee-directors

193 Roy Green, *Management Matters in Australia: Just how productive are we? Findings from the Australian Management Practices and Productivity global benchmarking project*, Department of innovation, Industry, Science and Research, November 2009, https://industry.gov.au/industry/OtherReportsandStudies/Documents/ManagementMattersinAustraliaReport.pdf

194 Swan, 'Restoring class balance'.

195 Paul Sakkal, 'Up where Cazaly?', *The Tocsin*, no. 1, June 2017, p. 29.

196 This section draws on Nick Dyrenfurth, *Curtin's Wish: Seven Big Ideas for a Better, Fairer Australia*, John Curtin Research Centre, Melbourne, 2018, https://www.curtinrc.org/curtins-wish and Nick Dyrenfurth, 'TAFE should no longer be the poor cousin to university', *The Age*, 27 January 2019, https://www.theage.com.au/national/tafe-should-no-longer-be-the-poor-cousin-to-university-20190123-p50t1u.html.

197 Quoted from Cater, 'UK Labour luminary Maurice Glasman unimpressed by ALP's efforts'.

198 This section draws on Dyrenfurth, *Curtin's Wish*.

199 Graham White, 'Not just a number: Defining full employment', *The Conversation*, 10 July 2013, https://theconversation.com/not-just-a-number-defining-full-employment-15248

200 Kim Carr, 'Back to the Future', *The Tocsin*, no. 3, December 2017, p. 23.

201 Adam Slonim and Nick Dyrenfurth, *Artificial Intelligence and the Future of Work*, John Curtin Research Centre Report, Melbourne, 2019, p. 10.

202 See Stuart Macintyre, *Winners and Losers: the pursuit of social justice in Australian history*, Allen & Unwin, Sydney, 1985.

203 Dawson, 'We're not all postmaterialists now', p. 9.

204 This section draws on Dyrenfurth, *Curtin's Wish*.

205 Quoted in Frank Bongiorno, *The People's Party: Victorian Labor and the Radical Tradition, 1875-1914*, Melbourne University Publishing, Carlton, 1994, p. 6.

206 George Orwell, 'The prevention of Literature', *Polemic*, no. 2, January 1946,

https://www.orwellfoundation.com/the-orwell-foundation/orwell/essays-and-other-works/the-prevention-of-literature/.

207 Pabst, *The Story of Our Country*, p. 21.

208 Tim Soutphommasane, *Reclaiming Patriotism: Nation-Building for Australian Progressives*, Cambridge University Press, Melbourne, 2009, p. 137.

209 Nick Dyrenfurth, *A Powerful influence on Australian affairs: a New History of the AWU*, Melbourne University Press, Melbourne, 2017, p. 3.

210 Quoted in Dyrenfurth, *Heroes and Villains*, p. 114.

211 ibid, p. 118.

212 ibid, p. 112.

213 This section draws on Dyrenfurth, *Heroes and Villains*, pp. 233-36.

214 ibid, p. 230.

215 Quoted in Nick Dyrenfurth, *Mateship: A Very Australian History*, Scribe, Melbourne, 2015, p. 136.

216 ibid, p. 183.

217 Bill Shorten, 'Address to the Australian 2014 Economic and Social Outlook Conference', 3 July 2014, https://www.billshorten.com.au/address-to-the-australian-2014-economic-and-social-outlook-conference

218 Michael Cooney, 'Seizing our Republican moment', *The Tocsin*, no. 2, October 2017, pp. 23.

219 Anthony Albanese, 'Address to Labor Caucus', Canberra, 30 May 2019, https://anthonyalbanese.com.au/address-to-labor-caucus-canberra-thursday-30-may-2019

220 The following section draws on Nick Dyrenfurth, 'Labor's damaged Right faction must renew', *The Saturday Paper*, 18 April 2015, https://www.thesaturdaypaper.com.au/opinion/topic/2015/04/18/labors-damaged-right-faction-must-renew/14292792001770

221 Adrian Pabst, ''Interregnum: the Fall and Rise of European Social Democracy, *The Tocsin*, no. 7, July 2019, p. 16.

222 Jon Cruddas, 'The Choice before One Nation Labour - to Transact or Transform', George Lansbury Memorial Lecture, London, 7 November 2013, https://www.newstatesman.com/politics/2013/11/jon-cruddass-george-lansbury-memorial-lecture-full-text

223 Janet McCalman, 'The New Precariat', *The Tocsin*, no. 1, June 2017, p. 17.

www.ingramcontent.com/pod-product-compliance
Lightning Source LLC
Chambersburg PA
CBHW070332270326
41926CB00017B/3848